PRAISE FOR

black and white BIBLE, black and blue wife

Ruth Tucker's historical and biblical scholarship has informed my own journey and that of countless egalitarians. In this book, however, her pedagogy is a story of abuse—her own. It is as powerful as it is personal, exposing the perils of a patriarchal reading of Scripture. Because Ruth's experiences are all too common, *Black and White Bible, Black and Blue Wife* is essential reading for pastors, seminarians, counselors, NGO workers, and indeed anyone who believes God speaks to us from the pages of Scripture.

> Dr. Mimi Haddad,
> president of Christians for Biblical Equality
> (www.cbeinternational.org)

I first knew Ruth Tucker as a colleague when she was much closer to the beginning of the story she recounts in this book. Ironically (or providentially), it was when she joined a team of women scholars working on a volume whose subtitle was *Facing the Challenge of Gender Reconciliation*. In *Black and White Bible, Black and Blue Wife*, she recounts the messy but also redemptive details of her own struggle with domestic violence—a topic that, one way or another, affects us all. This is a very courageous account that should motivate readers to action, even as it may disturb them.

> Mary Stewart Van Leeuwen,
> professor (emerita) of psychology,
> Eastern University

This book could save the lives of women trapped by domestic abuse. By courageously reliving in print years of degrading violence at the hands of her "Christian leader" ex-husband, Professor Ruth A. Tucker exposes a problem of epic proportions that tragically exists unchecked behind closed doors within evangelicalism. Worse yet, she demonstrates how such violence is actually fueled by so-called Christian theology that empowers men with authority and privilege over women and children under the guise of "husbandly headship," "servant leadership," and calls for "wifely submission." At great personal cost, Tucker drives a stake in the ground, insisting that abusive behavior is both unacceptable and indeed criminal. Her book is nothing less than a damning indictment of the church's tendency to justify or turn a blind eye to abuses happening within our own ranks. It is a prophetic call to rethink our theology of male and female. The church belongs on the forefront in the battle to root out and end abuse, to provide safe haven for the abused, and to see to it that abusers are brought to justice.

CAROLYN CUSTIS JAMES,
author of *Malestrom: Manhood Swept into the Currents of a Changing World*

black and white
BIBLE,
black and blue
wife

Other Books by Ruth A. Tucker

*From Jerusalem to Irian Jaya: A Biographical
History of Christian Missions*

*Daughters of the Church: Women and Ministry from New
Testament Times to the Present* (with Walter Liefeld)

*Private Lives of Pastor's Wives: From the
Reformation to the Present*

*Guardians of the Great Commission: The
Story of Women in Modern Missions*

*The Christian Speaker's Treasury: A
Sourcebook of Anecdotes and Quotes*

*Another Gospel: Alternative Religions
and the New Age Movement*

Stories of Faith: Daily Devotions from the Family of God

Women in the Maze: Questions and Answers on Biblical Equality

*Multiple Choices: Making Wise Decisions
in a Complicated World*

The Family Album: Portraits of Family Life through the Centuries

Seasons of Motherhood: A Garden of Memories

Not Ashamed: The Story of Jews for Jesus

*Walking Away from Faith: Unraveling the
Mystery of Belief and Unbelief*

God Talk: Cautions for Those Who Hear the Voice of God

*Left Behind in a Megachurch World: How God
Works Through Ordinary Churches*

Leadership Reconsidered: Becoming a Person of Influence

Parade of Faith: A Biographical History of the Christian Church

*The Biographical Bible: Exploring the Biblical
Narrative from Adam and Eve to John of Patmos*

*Dynamic Women of the Bible: What We Can
Learn from Their Surprising Stories*

*Black and White Bible, Black and Blue Wife: My
Story of Finding Hope after Domestic Abuse*

black and white
BIBLE,
black and blue
wife

My Story of Finding Hope after Domestic Abuse

RUTH A. TUCKER

ZONDERVAN

Black and White Bible, Black and Blue Wife
Copyright © 2016 by Ruth A. Tucker

This title is also available as a Zondervan ebook. Visit www.zondervan.com/ebooks.

This title is also available in a Zondervan audio edition. Visit www.zondervan.fm.

Requests for information should be addressed to:
Zondervan, 3900 *Sparks Dr. SE, Grand Rapids, Michigan 49546*

Library of Congress Cataloging-in-Publication Data

Names: Tucker, Ruth, 1945-
Title: Black and white Bible, black and blue wife : my story of finding hope after
    domestic abuse / Ruth A. Tucker.
Description: Grand Rapids: Zondervan, 2016. | Includes bibliographical references.
Identifiers: LCCN 2015033006 | ISBN 9780310524984 (softcover)
Subjects: LCSH: Sex crimes—Religious aspects—Christianity. | Marriage—Religious
    aspects—Christianity. | Sex role—Religious aspects—Christianity. | Family
    violence—Religious aspects—Christianity | Interpersonal relations—Religious
    aspects—Christianity | Tucker, Ruth, 1945-
Classification: LCC BV4596.A2 T83 2016 | DDC 261.8/327—dc23 LC record available at
    http://lcnn.loc.gov/2015033006

Cover design: *John Hamilton Design*
Cover photo: © *Michael Engman / GettyImages.com*
Interior design: *Denise Froehlich*

Printed in the United States of America

16 17 18 19 20 21 / DHV / 20 19 18 17 16 15 14 13 12 11 10 9 8 7 6 5 4 3 2 1

In memory of
Deana

These slightly altered lines are from
the first and final stanzas
of a rare and treasured 1888 volume
that I keep on my desk.

The Death of the Flowers
by
William Cullen Bryant

The melancholy days are come, the saddest of the year,
Of wailing winds, and naked woods, and
meadows brown and sere . . .
And then I think of one who in her youthful beauty died,
The fair meek blossom that grew up and faded by my side.
In the cold moist earth we laid her, when the forests cast the leaf,
And we wept that one so lovely should have a life so brief.

This book was both easy and traumatic to write.
There are things here
which I had very effectively buried
under layers of emotional scar tissue.
The process of tearing it away was
in some cases pleasurable
and in others deeply disturbing.
But it was always liberating.

PETER GODWIN, *MUKIWA: A WHITE BOY IN AFRICA*

contents

introduction

Opening the Curtain of Domestic Violence

I had a woman who was in a church that I served, and she was being subject to some abuse, and I told her, I said, "All right, what I want you to do is, every evening I want you to get down by your bed just as he goes to sleep, get down by the bed, and when you think he's just about asleep, you just pray and ask God to intervene, not out loud, quietly," but I said, "You just pray there." And I said, "Get ready because he may get a little more violent, you know, when he discovers this." And sure enough, he did. She came to church one morning with both eyes black. And she was angry at me and at God and the world, for that matter. And she said, "I hope you're happy." And I said, "Yes ma'am, I am." And I said, "I'm sorry about that, but I'm very happy."[1]

The reason he was happy, the Reverend Paige Patterson (then president of the Southern Baptist Convention) explained to a large conference audience in 2000, was that the man, after hearing his wife praying, came to church, and when the invitation was given, "he was the first one down to the front . . . And remember, when nobody else can help, God can."

Thirteen years before that, in 1987, I scheduled an appointment with the president of Trinity Evangelical Divinity School, Dr. Ken Meyer. I had asked for the meeting to inform him that later in the week I would be separating from my husband. I was apologetic for the embarrassment this would bring Trinity, and I was prepared to suggest two other professors who would be able to finish my courses for the remainder of the term. In no more than a sentence, I explained that my husband was violent and had beaten me on many occasions.

"Why haven't you come to me earlier?" Dr. Meyer asked. "Are you okay? Do you have a support network back in Grand Rapids? How is your son doing? Of course, you're doing the right thing to escape with your son." And then, without so much as a "poor baby," he launched into a lecture. In the many years he had served as a pastor, he had repeatedly counseled abused women to get out of their dangerous domestic situations. They took his advice until their husbands wept and apologized and pleaded for reconciliation, promising never to beat them again. But the violence always continued.

When I told him my husband would never apologize, he shook his head and said with a sigh, "Mark my words, he will." President Meyer insisted that I must separate for at least six months until my husband underwent serious counseling, and perhaps even then we should not be reconciled. Such violence is pathological, and a class in anger management often serves as little more than a Band-Aid.

Ken Meyer was spot-on in his assessment. With the help of a singularly compassionate attorney and an understanding minister at our church, my son and I escaped to safety. Through the court, I was granted a restraining order, separate maintenance, and sole custody of Carlton. Soon thereafter, my husband indeed apologized and agreed to joint counseling sessions with a Bible church minister whose small church was on a country road forty minutes north of Grand Rapids. It proved to be very ineffective. My husband and I were not reconciled. Three years later, I received a call from an attorney in New Jersey, informing me that my husband, whose whereabouts neither my son nor I had known, was suing for divorce. I did not contest.

In the decades since we escaped, friends, acquaintances, and even publishers have urged me to write my story. Why not? Writing is my primary profession. But the pain of reliving those years has always stood in the way. More than that, humiliation. Few can comprehend the depth of shame that still lingers. And not just the shame of being married to an abusive minister, but also the awful acknowledgment of my own complicity—the failure to report my husband to law enforcement when his crimes involved an innocent foster child.

"Your wifely submission [by not reporting him] was the right thing to do," the Bible church minister assured me. It was not. What I failed to do was self-serving and terribly wrong, indeed, perhaps deadly wrong. By my very knowledge, I was an accomplice, and I will be haunted by that crime for the rest of my life.

Despite the dread in writing and publicizing my story, I was prodded into action by a news report I saw in mid-September 2014. A security camera had captured an NFL player hitting his fiancée in an elevator, knocking her to the floor and then dragging her limp body out of the elevator door. Ray Rice, the perpetrator, had previously undergone sessions in anger management. What good had it done? Should I have been shocked to learn that his fiancée married him some months after the incident?

President Paige Patterson counseled a victim of domestic violence to kneel by the bed and pray. President Ken Meyer counseled a victim to get away from the perpetrator, warning that violent abusers are often left unchanged by counseling.

If this volume saves even one woman from further domestic abuse, my dread in writing will have been worth it. I do not speak as a lone voice. With me are historical and contemporary women whose stories have shaken me even as they have sustained me. More than that, I am bolstered by the Bible and its honest telling of terrible transgressions—transgressions involving God's own people. Scripture serves as a blueprint for anyone today who opens the curtain on a marriage and reveals ugly secrets. But even more, its pages present in plain sight a model for mutuality in marriage.

Here in this volume, two themes are balanced: *black-and-white Bible* and *black-and-blue wife*. During his violent rages, my ex-husband often hurled biblical texts at me, as though the principal tenet of Scripture was, "Wives, submit to your husbands." He spit the words out, repeatedly beating me over the head, at least figuratively, with his black-and-white Bible. His hitting and punching and slamming me against doors and furniture, however, were anything but figurative. Nor were his terror-loaded threats. I felt trapped and feared for my life, while outwardly disguising bruises with long sleeves and clever excuses, pretending that ours was a happy marriage.

1

moving beyond headship debates

Finding Common Ground in Storytelling

I was wound up. An energizer bunny. Tingling with excitement—maybe even a tad nervous. It was seven o'clock on the night of October 25, 1995. The setting, Pierce Chapel at Wheaton College. As I looked out over the crowd, it appeared as though all nine hundred seats were filled—students standing up and down the outer aisles and in the rear, stretching as far as I could see into the vestibule. The event had been well publicized. Though not necessarily the *mother* of all debates or the *debate of the decade*, word had obviously gotten out. I was there to face off against Dr. John Piper. The plan was not for a formal debate. Rather, we were each given an allotted amount of time to speak to the question, Should marriage be based on a model of mutual submission and equality or on a model of male headship?

I look over the text of my address today, two decades later, and nod my head in agreement, while scolding myself here and there for using the passive voice or a weak verb. But the position I took then has changed very little. Yet I wonder about the value of such debates. Would it have been better if John and I had each sat down in an easy chair on that stage and told our stories, while at the same time speaking to biblical and theological issues? But that was not the format. If I were to debate today, I would say some of the same things but take a very different approach.

And today I would certainly hope that any thought of victory would be excised from my mind. It felt good when students cheered, but as I recall, most of the students seemed to have come with their minds already made up. The majority of those who supported mutuality in marriage no doubt thought I won the debate, and vice versa. When we contemplate Christian marriage today, the stakes are high. Little is accomplished by winning or losing in a public forum.

It was perhaps mere coincidence that John Piper and I each presented our positions in ten points, mine in the form of questions. My first eight questions briefly answered common misunderstandings related to mutual submission and headship in marriage. My ninth question asked if mutual submission is supported by Scripture. A quick word count of that twenty-year-old document shows that more than half of my entire presentation was a response to this single question. I began with Adam and Eve, skipped right ahead to Jesus, and then zeroed in on the apostle Paul.

Despite our ten-point similarity, John Piper and I approached the topic from very different angles. He did not go through various biblical passages to make his case, though had he been inclined, he was certainly capable of doing so. Rather, he approached the subject from the top down. I zeroed in on Scripture that dealt with women and men in marriage. His emphasis was on God's supremacy, as is indicated by selected sentences from his text:

My own personal mission statement is to spread a passion for the supremacy of God in all things . . . God does not like being taken for granted. The very reason for creation is God's going public for the glory of God . . . God has designed human beings to magnify His glory . . . Since my mission here is to spread a passion for the supremacy of God in all things for the joy of all people, I commend to you this complementary view of marriage and family rather than an egalitarian one.[1]

It may not be too simplistic to suggest that the differences he and I demonstrated in the Wheaton debate go to the very heart of the wider evangelical debate on women's equality in the church and in marriage. Of course, God is sovereign. That is a given for anyone who upholds historic orthodoxy. But is God's supremacy the starting point in dealing with gender roles, particularly the relationship between husband and wife?

That God's supremacy should be the foundation for a husband's role in marriage is not necessarily an obvious conclusion. There are certainly other biblical truths that seem far more appropriate, including the comforting passage in Hebrews 13 (quoting from Deuteronomy and Psalms) in which God says, "'Never will I leave you; never will I forsake you.' So we say with confidence, 'The Lord is my helper; I will not be afraid.'" Here is a passage that reflects on God and at the same time profoundly speaks to the mutuality between a husband and wife. The Lord is my "helper," as husbands and wives are helpers to each other.

It is true that the apostle Paul asserts that the husband is the "head" of the wife (Ephesians 5:23). This statement, however, is surely not a slam dunk for the claim of male privilege. The verdict is still out on the meaning of "head." Indeed, *kephalē*, the Greek word translated "head," has been endlessly debated by biblical scholars. Our contemporary usage suggests the meaning is "ruler," but from the biblical context, the concept of "source" (an equally valid rendering of *kephalē*) is actually more fitting. But however *kephalē* is defined, when it is used for the husband, it is always in the context of Christ as head of the church. Indeed, this metaphor is an absolutely jaw-dropping concept.

We sometimes read right past these words from Paul's letter to the Ephesians: "Husbands, love your wives, just as Christ loved the church and gave himself up for her." Really? The standard is impossible. Christ gave himself up for the church by submitting to crucifixion. The husband's role is obviously to be read metaphorically. No husband is expected to die on a cross for his wife. Still, the benchmark is very high. The great eighteenth-century Methodist theologian John Fletcher clearly understood that. Late in life, he married Mary Bosanquet, a noted preacher in her own right. His words are instructive. Gathered with friends after the ceremony, he read from Ephesians 5: "Husbands, love your wives, just as Christ loved the church." His spontaneous comments are most revealing: "My God, what a task! Help me, my friends, by your prayers to fulfil it. As Christ loved the church! He laid aside his glory for her!"[2]

When I think of a husband laying aside his glory for his wife, Robertson McQuilkin immediately comes to mind. Although the back cover of his book *A Promise Kept* identifies him first as a homemaker, most people know him as having served for more than two decades as the president of Columbia International University in Columbia, South Carolina. Much to the chagrin of the university's board of trustees, he quit at the height of his career to become a full-time homemaker. His wife, Muriel, had been diagnosed with Alzheimer's disease in 1981. By 1990, her condition had deteriorated to the point that she was becoming agitated and fearful unless he was with her. He had not promised "till death do us part" to the university. To Muriel, however, he had. So he laid aside his glory as a university president to become a caregiver for Muriel.

Five years into his "retirement," he reflected on the course their lives had taken: "Seventeen summers ago, Muriel and I began our journey into the twilight. It's midnight now . . . Yet, in her silent world, Muriel is so content, so lovable. If Jesus took her home, how I would miss her gentle, sweet presence."[3]

That gentle presence, however, was at times interrupted by utter frustration. On one occasion before Muriel began wearing diapers, she had an accident in the bathroom and Robertson was trying to clean her up. She was pushing him away, clumsily trying to take care of herself. He told her to stop. She ignored him. In exasperation, he slapped the calf of her leg. "She was startled," he writes. "I was, too. Never in our 44 years of marriage had I ever so much as touched her in anger . . . But now, when she needed me most . . ."[4]

Now, when she needed me most . . . The reader can almost hear the choke in his voice.

What an incredible illustration of Christ's love for the church—a husband's unconditional love for a wife. Of course, Paul goes on to speak directly to the wife (as we will later discuss).

How sad it is when a Christian man cannot say, "Never in our years of marriage had I ever so much as touched her in anger." What if, rather, the husband beats his wife in anger?

During the debate with John Piper, I addressed the matter of a wife submitting to her husband even if he physically abuses her. I told how Elisabeth Elliot had spoken to a large audience of women (primarily seminary wives) at Trinity Evangelical Divinity School. After her talk, one of the wives asked, "Should a woman remain in a home where she is being physically abused by her husband?" In her remarks, Elliot pointed the audience to 1 Peter 2, which speaks of slaves being beaten. She then made reference to the next chapter: "*In the same way, you women must accept the authority of your husbands.*" With that, she added a troubling comment: "I don't think that requires a woman necessarily to stay in a home where she is literally being physically beaten to death. But on the other hand, it might." Were there any young women in that packed room that evening who only heard the words "on the other hand, it might"?

After this illustration, my allotted time was up. In my closing remarks, I said, "Scripture and good judgment tell us that a pattern of mutual submission and equal partnership is the best way we can effectively serve the Lord in a marriage relationship."

I did not tell my listeners about the years of abuse I had endured and my own terrifying dread of being literally beaten to death. I was married to a Bible church minister. There were dozens of incidents I could have referred to. One in particular, however, might have caught their attention more than others as it related to my work as a professor. Since 1982, I had been flying from our home in Grand Rapids to Chicago's O'Hare Airport to teach at Trinity for two or three days each week for fall and spring quarters. The routine worked well. Our son was in middle school, active in sports, and managing to keep on top of his paper route.

There had been many violent instances throughout the nineteen years of our marriage. On numerous occasions, my ex-husband beat me or threw me against a desk or onto the floor—always behind closed doors and most often when our son was out of the house. I was convinced I was becoming better at managing these outbursts by strictly avoiding certain subjects and being alert to his ominous moods, brewing and portentous as they were.

It was a cold West Michigan evening in March. Spring quarter at Trinity had begun a week earlier. I recognized my husband's mood before we had even sat down for the evening meal. When we finished eating, I tidied up the kitchen, took my books and notes, and went upstairs while he watched his usual TV programs and Carlton did homework nearby, listening in as he typically did.

After an hour or so, I heard my husband's footsteps on the stairs. I stiffened, dreading the worst. He entered our bedroom where I was hunkered down and then, seemingly out of the blue, with not so much as a segue into the topic, demanded to know my interpretation of a particular biblical passage that related to women. I explained that I was very busy in course preparation and did not wish to discuss the matter, particularly because I knew it would create problems. He proceeded to give me his interpretation of the passage. When I remained silent and refused to agree with him, he became irate and began very loudly to threaten me and exclaim that he would not let me fly to O'Hare in the morning. He yanked me from where I was sitting, my papers flying in every direction.

Hearing his father shouting, Carlton was up the stairs two steps at a time. It was not the first time he sought to defend me. Normally, his crying out at his father put an end to violence. But not this time. My husband demanded he leave the room while at the same time squeezing my arms with all his might and viciously shaking me. Carlton did leave. He raced back to his own room and grabbed two knives, one no more than a hard plastic toy, the other a Swiss Army knife he had managed to open before returning to confront his father. At twelve, Carlton was tall and lanky, but no match for his six-foot-two father, who could do a hundred push-ups without breaking a sweat.

When I saw the knives, I screamed for Carlton to get out, but within seconds my husband had thrown him to the floor, taken the knives, and was coming at me again. In a second, Carlton got back up and tackled his father, crying out at the top of his lungs. And then somehow amid the mayhem, it ended. My husband left the room still raging, ordering Carlton to come downstairs with him.

The next afternoon I was in Deerfield, greeting students in my classroom and wearing a turtleneck and blazer that conveniently covered the bruises—black-and-blue finger marks on my upper arms. I had taught the course before, and once I was into my rhythm and a lively discussion was under way, I was in another world. After the class ended in the late afternoon and all the students had checked in with me on term projects, I gathered my books and notes and began making my way over to the little apartment on campus where I stayed. My *real* life flooded over me, covering me like a shroud—like a shroud of pitch-black, oily fright. A quick call home to Carlton relieved the tension. But the situation seemed hopeless. Our little family was a complete mess. Where would it all end?

There are many underlying factors to consider in attempting to understand why a husband would beat and terrorize his wife. I'm certain a psychiatrist could write an entire volume on my ex-husband. But from my vantage point, his perspective on male supremacy and female submission was front and center. He repeatedly quoted Scripture to defend his headship and to enforce my unconditional obligation to submit—from "the kitchen to the bedroom." He might have added to that list my home office where I prepared lectures. His rule was absolute and final—most notably during his violent moods. *Black-and-white Bible, black-and-blue wife.*

Why didn't I just pack up and leave with Carlton? That's a complicated question that will be dealt with throughout this volume. Perhaps a more appropriate question that relates specifically to this chapter is, Why didn't I tell this very story to that full house at Wheaton? It's a story the audience—students, staff, faculty, and visitors—needed to hear. I was a professor, like my fellow professors at Wheaton. The crowd could relate to that. And here I was, a woman, a wife, a mother, standing before them. I was exhibit A.

In fact, what if the forum for that evening at Wheaton College would have been not a debate but a storytelling forum—a session during which John Piper and I simply sat down and interacted with each other about real people and about ourselves. We could have done that. We knew each other. I spoke one Sunday night about missions history at his church in Minneapolis. I was welcomed into his home. I commend him for his bestselling book, *Desiring God* and for his active involvement in missions outreach around the world. And he has commended me. In fact, in January of 1984, he wrote (now posted online), "Noël and I are reading together in the evening Ruth Tucker's book *From Jerusalem to Irian Jaya: A Biographical History of Christian Missions* (Zondervan, 1983). Then we pray together." In 1993, he made reference again to his and Noël's having read that book together nine years earlier.

Instead of debating, he could have related experiences of counseling married couples in his ministry, and he might have talked about how he and Noël work through issues. I might have told stories about my parents' marriage and revealed details of my own marriage breakdown. Imagine the impact we could have had on those students.

Some, of course, prefer debates and proof texting. But I would remind them that storytelling is the stuff of the Bible. True, there is nothing wrong with debates. We learn a lot from them. The debate over headship, however, has become rancorous in recent years, often sounding very un-Christian.

But is it possible, I wonder, to deal with some very touchy matters with graciousness? Can we come together as a Christian community and recognize that the doctrine of male headship has sometimes been used as a cover to perpetrate violence against women? At the same time, can we come together in an understanding that marriage based on mutual submission is a biblical model—a valid interpretation of Scripture? I acknowledge that the headship model is *a valid way to interpret the Bible*. I certainly do not believe it is the most faithful interpretation, particularly in light of the central themes of Scripture, but I would never claim it has no biblical basis at all and is simply pulled out of a magician's hat.

I truly believe we are at a turning point. We can keep on going as we have previously done, debating the issues, each side marshaling texts and claiming to win the argument. Or we can find a new way to interact with civility and respect. Can we find common ground in all of the Bible's stories, and not just the Adam and Eve account? Let's talk about Sarah and Abraham, and Rebekah and Isaac, and Jacob and his wives. Let's talk about Naomi and Ruth and their plan to approach Boaz in the dark of night. Let's talk about Bathsheba and David, Mary and Joseph, Ananias and Sapphira. Can we as men and women who are seeking to serve God today benefit from their stories? We can, even as we recognize that their stories aren't so different from ours. Let's talk about them and their struggles. Let's talk about Ruth Tucker and domestic violence. Let's talk about Robertson McQuilkin and his painful confession and abiding love for Muriel.

I was moved to tears when I reread Robertson McQuilkin's story—for both Muriel and for him. Here is an intelligent, engaging, and capable woman lost in the depths of an awful disease. She has not yet begun to wear diapers, and he is in the bathroom trying to clean her up. As much as we want to turn away and close the bathroom door, we must leave it open for our own understanding of what marriage entails. We must picture that scene. It is an altogether pitiful and private moment. She in her sickness is pushing him away. Picture the mess. Picture it. She's trying to take care of herself. Of course she is. Doesn't everyone try to take care of themselves in such circumstances? But in her condition she can't. He tells her to stop; she doesn't. He raises his voice. She ignores him, pushing him away from her. He slaps her on the leg. Then the question that knifes right through him: "What have I done?"

He admits to that hasty slap in print. And then those haunting words of remorse: "Never in our 44 years of marriage had I ever so much as touched her in anger . . . But now, when she needed me most . . ."

Robertson McQuilkin's account of his marriage to Muriel is a profound illustration of a husband demonstrating Christ's love. But the reverse—a wife ministering to her husband in such circumstances, as often happens—is equally telling. Such love is not determined by gender or by one's particular view of male headship and mutual submission. "In sickness and in health" has meaning. In fact, this very vow had momentous implications for my second husband, John Worst. His first wife, also Ruth, was diagnosed with stage 3 ovarian cancer in 1995. She enjoyed four years of moderately good health between surgeries. But the surgeries could only do so much, and by 1998, surgery and chemo only prolonged what doctors had confirmed was a terminal illness. Soon after that, John requested early retirement from his vocation as a professor of music at Calvin College.

By the summer of 1999, though still alert and quick-witted, Ruth, as John describes her, was hardly more than "a bag of bones." This particularly hit home one evening when he heard her whimpering in the bathroom—"almost the sound of a kitten." He got up from his chair and raced across the room and opened the door. She had fallen. He picked her up in his arms, no heft at all.

Shortly after that, John arranged for Ruth to go to a home environment at a nearby hospice facility, where he would be able to spend his days with her. She had reached the point where he no longer had peace about her even attempting to walk on her own. She needed to be where she could have round-the-clock care. They arrived and settled in to the nicely furnished bedroom. After eating and spending some time together, he was preparing to leave for the night. Only then did he realize how deeply sad she was. Sadness, of course, was ever-present for both of them, especially toward the end. But this was different. He paused. He stood looking at her in silence.

"Would you like to come back home?" John whispered. Ruth nodded. So her clothes and books and magazines and personal items were packed up, and they returned to their condo. The days that followed were not easy, often causing him to wonder if he had made the right choice to bring her home. Hospice nurses stopped by, but he was in charge. Looking back, he knows that, despite those distressing and unpredictable days, he had made the right choice. John now speaks of this most personal and private care he was able to give Ruth as a *sacrament* of duty. During that time and throughout her illness, he fulfilled vows that are too often taken lightly. He is quick to point out, however, that each couple must make these decisions together—that there is no one-size-fits-all in living through a painful ordeal such as he and Ruth endured.

In October 2000, John married again. Myra had been a colleague at Calvin, and he had fallen hopelessly in love, knowing she had been diagnosed with pancreatic cancer. She was a friend of mine, and whenever I'd see her at church, she was always her cheery self and acted as though she was perfectly healthy. But her remission lasted only so long. The marriage was short—just a little more than three years. She commented to me on several occasions that her marriage to John—her only marriage—was the best time of her life. Once again, John performed a sacrament of duty as he cared for her to the very end.

The relationship between a husband and wife is surely not defined by debates. A marriage—a God-honoring marriage—is lived out *till death do us part.* Its deepest significance comes when modeled on Christ, who gave himself up for us. Stories show us the way. Indeed, stories, far more than biblical proof texting, show us how to work through the tough times of life. They also show us where both sides of the debate can meet on common ground.

Robertson McQuilkin's story, John's stories, and even my own serve to remind us that the most profound way we exegete Scripture is through our lives. For McQuilkin, there would be times when he, even more than I, surely felt himself being flooded over and covered by a shroud—a shroud of pitch-black, oily despair. In fact, he writes that there was a stretch of time when he truly feared he might be heading into his own midnight.

He could mouth the words that he trusted God—that God was in control of his life and of Muriel's, but he could not process the depth of his pain emotionally and spiritually. "The blows of life," he wrote, "had left me numb—my dearest slipping from me, my eldest son snatched away in a tragic accident, my life's work abandoned at its peak." Depression engulfed him. His love for God "frozen over."[5]

There was one incident amid this darkness that, small as it was, revived his depleted spirit. He found his way back to God and emotional stability, not through the hymn lyrics, "showers of blessings," but rather through what could only be described as tiny teardrops of God's tender mercies. "Sometimes the happy doesn't bubble up with joy," he reflected, "but rains down gently with tears."[6]

The day was gloomy, not necessarily the weather, but the day as a state of mind. It was the morning after Valentine's Day 1995. The day before had been the anniversary of their marriage engagement. Robertson was exercising, as he normally did, on his stationary bicycle at the foot of Muriel's bed. She awakened and spoke for the first time in months. The word was "love," three times repeated. They were words he had so many times spoken to her during her seemingly endless silence. But he was astounded and rushed to embrace her, begging her, pleading with her to assure him: "You really do love me, don't you?" She responded in the affirmative with the only words that her lips and her enfeebled mind could form: "I'm nice"—the last words she ever spoke.[7]

From her, Robertson had received a Valentine—teardrops of tender mercies.

Muriel died in 2003 at the age of eighty-one. Robertson had first met her in college decades earlier, where he remembered her as "delightful, smart, and gifted" and "more fun than you can imagine."[8] Prior to her final illness, Muriel had taught at Columbia International University, was a conference speaker, and had her own radio talk show—smart and gifted. Soon after her death, Robertson wrote: "For 55 years Muriel was flesh of my flesh, bone of my bone. So it's like a ripping of my flesh and deeper—my very bones, but there is also profound gratitude . . . I've delighted in recalling happy memories."[9] Indeed, a marriage of mutuality.

In 2005, Robertson married again. Dr. Deborah Jones Sink was then a professor of nursing at the University of South Carolina. She was a leader in her field and had previously been the owner of First Place Leadership Development and also vice president of Goebel Marketing Associates. She and Robertson brought together a blended family of nine children.

Robertson's marriage to Muriel (and now to Deborah) is a narrative that should be part of the canon of every Christian storybook, told again and again to the young and old who find themselves falling in love in that perilous Garden of Paradise. There is a serpent close by that wants us to believe that true love comes naturally and is all about sex and sweetness. "Marriage is easy," the serpent assures—simple, straightforward, blissful, and bright. We too easily take a bite out of the apple that leads to banishment. The love takes flight, and marriage is irretrievably broken. The sacred vows carved into the Tree of Life have been covered over with lichen and are no longer visible.

> *To have and to hold from this day forward,*
> *for better for worse,*
> *for richer for poorer,*
> *in sickness and in health,*
> *to love and to cherish,*
> *till death us do part.*

2

pollution in paradise

A Snake in the Garden of Perfection

> So hand in hand they passed, the loveliest pair that ever since in love's embraces met—Adam, the goodliest man of men since born his sons; the fairest of her daughters Eve.
>
> **JOHN MILTON, *PARADISE LOST***

My attraction to the story of Adam and Eve has found its habitation in the heart of imagination and among questions rather than answers. As a gardener, I close my eyes and wonder about a garden without blight, without tomato hornworm, and trees without emerald ash borer. But I wonder most about the man and the woman. How do two individuals communicate when there is no memory, when there is no past, when there are no parents or siblings? Did they invent their own language, or were they created with words?

When I contemplate this Garden of Eden, this Paradise, I wonder if it is appropriate to see it as a metaphor for falling in love. It has all the elements. The perfect setting is created just for that perfectly created male and female.

They are in love, and they need no words. Everything between them is perfect in that perfect garden. They know nothing about thunder and hail, arguments, frustrations, hard work, pain, and old age. They know nothing of violence and death and the land of Nod, the region where a firstborn son—a murderer—will live out the remainder of his life. They have little awareness of anything else going on around them except their own love. They hang on each other like succulent drops of sweet wine dripping from pregnant clusters of luscious grapes. They lie together and sleep at night, entwined like a vine around a tree.

Perhaps like the lady lover in Song of Songs, Eve teases with erotic sensuality: "Let him kiss me with the kisses of his mouth—for your love is more delightful than wine" (1:2). She describes herself almost as we might imagine evocative phrases on a dating site: "Dark am I, yet lovely . . . dark like the tents of Kedar" (1:5). This lady lover is just like the dazzling, dark Eve.

Her steamy style, when whispered by Eve, is sure to excite Adam: "My beloved is to me a sachet of myrrh resting between my breasts . . . Our bed is verdant" (1:13, 16). No erotic craving is left unspoken between either one of this Song of Songs pair, even as we imagine Adam responding:

> *I slept but my heart was awake.*
> *Listen! My beloved is knocking:*
> *"Open to me, my sister, my darling,*
> *my dove, my flawless one." (5:2)*

If we were to continue to allow Eve to whisper the words of the lady lover, her paraphrase would be equally erotic:

> *I belong to my beloved,*
> *and his desire is for me.*
> *Come, my beloved, let us wander through the garden;*
> *let us spend the night lying in the moonlit moss.*

Let us go early to the vineyards
to see if the vines have budded,
if their blossoms have opened,
and if the pomegranates are in bloom—
there I will give you my love. (7:10–12)

Adam and Eve are naked. The perfect undress for this infinitely romantic setting. One restriction, yes. But everything else is for their pleasure—as near to perfect as male and female could ever enjoy. They wander hand in hand along rippling streams, picking succulent, ripened mangos the size of her breasts, an offering to each other's lips, titillating their taste buds.

There is never a cross word between them as they stroll beneath the live oaks and palms, pushing aside blueberry bushes bowed down with juicy, plump delicacies. They recite poetry in the language of love. Romance, sweet nothings, breathless touching. Perfection. Perfection all around them, perfection in each other.

I was once in Eden, and I fell in love. "Found in the heart of the Adirondacks, in the middle of the 9-mile Schroon Lake sits a 49-acre Island where excitement and life change happen."[1] Word of Life Island was for me in 1967 a place of excitement where life change happened, oh yes.

The most dangerous circumstance in any woman's life is not walking, as I once did to the rhythm of heart-pounding fear, south on Giddings Avenue in the dark. It is the heart-pounding thrill of falling in love. Senseless infatuation. Tall, dark, and handsome, a perfect creature, an Adam, appearing almost out of nowhere. The setting on this island paradise was a large, screened meeting room above the boathouse. It was an informal gathering of college-and-career-age campers. The MC announced a little game. He called out Bible verse references, and anyone could stand and quote the verse. As a camp counselor, I waited for others. When no one stood, I took my turn. Finally, it was just me, and when I didn't know the verse, this six-foot-two stranger nailed it every time.

How romantic is that!

For a single male fundamentalist in the late 1960s, a single woman quoting Bible verses beats succulent, ripened mangos hands down. When the meeting was over, the stranger found me, and romance quickly blossomed in our very own little Eden. We managed to get off the island that week for long walks and talks. I hung on every word this most alluring specimen of humanity uttered. Here I was, an unsophisticated farm girl from northern Wisconsin, being held in the arms of a debonair gentleman from New York City. We were in the paradise of the Adirondack Mountains. It was the Garden of Eden.

(I know this because the great American artist and founder of the Hudson River School, Thomas Cole, painted Garden of Eden scenes. One such landscape, completed in the late 1830s, was titled simply *Schroon Lake*.)

The Garden of Eden is where beguiling romance is born. All it takes is two perfect people swooning, whispering sweet nothings, finding no fault. The deception of perfection. Suddenly a snake slithers in the grass and comes onto the scene. Oh, how crafty is this clever creature. Sure, there have been red flags and warnings, but the serpent casts doubts, soothes an uneasy conscience, dismisses an unsure query. Like Eve, I did not ask hard questions. Suspicions and uncertainties disappeared like blossoms in the breeze. The lure of the forbidden fruit was irresistible. I ate the apple.

Next to Jezebel, Eve is the most maligned woman of the Bible. She was the temptress. She brought her husband into sin. Or was she the first example of a woman suffering domestic violence, Adam the perpetrator? She was, according to Jocelyn Andersen, author of *Woman Submit! Christians and Domestic Violence* and a domestic violence survivor herself. Author Kathryn Joyce highlights Andersen's unique take on Adam and Eve:

> The story of the Fall should not be seen as a prescription for marriage roles, [Andersen] argues, with women charged to follow men as punishment for acting outside the chain of

command, but rather as the first chapter in a long history of domestic violence of husband against wife. In Andersen's reading, the story of Adam and Eve is that of Adam's deadly betrayal of his wife: offering her up for punishment—the wages of eating the apple were death—rather than owning his blame for sin. Women have been responding in a sort of biblical battered wife syndrome, the "Eve Syndrome," ever since.[2]

I would not have come up with this interpretation myself, but that a man "ruling over" a woman (or a wife) would lead to domestic violence is not entirely off the mark, at least in many instances. On the other hand, the one does not necessarily follow the other. Parents "rule over" their children, making them do homework and forbidding them to play kickball in the street. But it does not follow that they also abuse this child. However, that a wife should be "ruled over" by a husband and punished if she does not obey (as a child is by parents) is surely not the message that comes from the creation account or any other biblical passage.

How, then, do we define domestic violence or abuse? Some writers, including sociologists and criminal justice experts, define the term broadly, as in "any act which *contravenes the rights* of another" or "the attempt of an individual or group to impose its will on others through any nonverbal, verbal, or physical means that inflict psychological or physical injury."[3]

I find such definitions fuzzy. They have the potential to turn almost any strong disagreement into abuse. A husband or wife uses harsh language. The wife tries to impose her will on the husband, and vice versa. Tempers flare. Feelings are hurt. It happens in a marriage and among siblings and friends. It happens *all the time* in politics. But do we muddy the discussion if we call it abuse?

Violence is obviously abuse, whether the wife is throwing dinner plates or the husband is ripping off cabinet doors. A one-time push or shove may not be, unless the wife is slammed into a kitchen counter or onto the floor. Demeaning criticism (particularly when it happens

33

repeatedly) is abuse and should not be tolerated in marriage or in any other setting.

If depicting Eve as a battered wife seems preposterous to some, so should be depicting Eve as a feminist. Yet that claim has sometimes been propounded by those holding a patriarchal position. In an online essay titled "Eve, the Original Feminist," Bryce Laliberte writes:

> The actual sins committed by Adam and Eve are also distinct. While both involved eating of the tree of life, Eve did so in order to "be as God, knowing good and evil" while Adam appears to have done so in order to please his woman. In other words, it appears that Eve was the first woman stricken by penis envy, and Adam was the first beta who failed to keep his woman in line by ruling over her . . . Patriarchy is a cultural response to the postlapsarian state. Without the fall, men would still be head of the relationship, but would find no need to "rule" . . . just as we might imagine an unfallen world where wives did the will of their husbands on the sole basis of their position and mutual love.[4]

Long before Laliberte was calling Eve the first feminist, John Milton in *Paradise Lost* was doing so, though without using the term. Before Eve is tempted by the serpent, she makes a proposition to Adam: "Let us divide our labours, thou where choice leads thee . . . while I in yonder Spring of Roses intermixt with Myrtle" (IX. 214–19).

Eve desires independence. Adam speaks against her reasoning, but she wins the argument: "And what is Faith, Love, Virtue unassayed [untried] alone, without exterior help sustained?" (IX. 335–36). So she goes off on her own, and that is where she meets the serpent. She sets the stage for all women after her to seek independence from their husbands.

In a chapter in *Recovering Biblical Manhood and Womanhood*, Raymond Ortlund Jr. interprets the passage more pointedly:

> What actually happened is full of meaning. Eve usurped Adam's headship and led the way into sin. And Adam . . . for his part, abandoned his post as head . . .

Isn't it striking that we fell upon an occasion of sex role reversal? Are we to repeat this confusion forever? Are we to institutionalize it in evangelicalism in the name of the God who condemned it in the beginning?[5]

Here we find a curious twist—that of Adam and Eve sinning before the fall, perhaps only seconds before eating the fruit but nonetheless before they actually ate it. As Ortlund sets it up, sex role reversal was "condemned" by God "in the beginning." So in his scenario, Adam and Eve sinned and fell under condemnation by reversing their roles before they sinned by disobeying God and eating the fruit. It is interesting that God does not bring up the matter of sex role reversal when he confronts them in the cool of the evening.

The biblical text itself speaks only of the sin of disobedience for eating the fruit, and God's charge against them is for that very sin. Nothing is said to Eve about "usurping Adam's headship" or to Adam about "abandoning his post as head."

How do Bible interpreters come up with the idea that male headship was instituted in the garden before the fall? That Adam was created before Eve, that Eve was his *helper*, and that Adam *named* Eve are claims used to defend this position. In many respects, these matters are distractions and altogether less than significant. One matter, however, I cannot leave unchallenged—a matter I find to be no less than exegetical mischief. To claim that God created the woman as *helper* and placed her as subordinate to the man is simply not accurate. At stake is the proper rendering of the Hebrew word *ēzer*, translated "helper" (and the phrase *ēzer kenegdo*, translated "helpmate" or "helper suitable"). Far from a place of subordination, *ēzer* is used in Scripture most frequently when associated with God and with male names. In Exodus 18:4, we see that Moses' son was named Eliezer because "my father's God was my helper" (*ēzer*). How well I remember the plaque in the farmhouse kitchen where I grew up: "The Lord is my helper. Whom shall I fear?"

But at the end of the day, it's tempting to call for a truce and plead with both sides to just leave Adam and Eve alone. Let them enjoy paradise for as long as it takes them to sin, and then let them have babies and till the soil. Sad news will come soon enough. For someone simply reading through the text, the murder of Abel at the hand of his brother, Cain, is what tears the heart out. Indeed, in a very real sense this account of murder, next to the crucifixion of Jesus, is the most searing story of the Bible. Garden romance all too quickly warps into homicidal reality.

For Adam and Eve, the giddy days of perfection and pure romance are barely a memory. So, too, for all of us. Troubles are only a temptation away. The garden is overrun with weeds, and the snake slithers through the grass. My Garden of Eden romance was filled with red flags, but that crafty serpent kept rational thinking at bay.

After the whirlwind romance in and around Schroon Lake, we waited a year to marry. It might seem like sufficient time to work out issues between us, but it wasn't. He was in New Jersey; I was at Baylor University in graduate school. The 1,636 miles that separated us were figuratively light-years away in marriage preparation. He visited my family in Wisconsin at Christmas; I visited his parents on Long Island during my spring break. We were briefly together again in June prior to our August wedding.

During our Texas–New Jersey separation, we talked frequently on the phone, and he sent letters that contained his own biblical commentaries on the subject of marriage—nothing that struck me as particularly controversial at the time. I saved all of his letters and packed them away in a box in our attic (that is, before his mother went into the trunk of my car parked in her driveway during our honeymoon, opened a large box, found the cache of letters, took them inside, opened every envelope, and read each one). That box (which I later retrieved from her) was one of the items that my ex-husband took, unbeknownst to me, at the time of our separation. Now as I am reflecting on our early relationship, I'm wondering if those letters were filled with warning signs of our future marriage breakdown.

During his visit at Christmas, he was determined to proceed with marriage plans. There was one major hurdle before us, however. Wifely obedience, you say? I don't remember that this issue even arose. The hurdle was my failure to sign on to his belief in six twenty-four-hour days of creation some six thousand years ago. Was he really making that a prerequisite for our getting married? I was stunned. A year earlier, one of my brainy college friends, who happened to be a strong Calvinist, suddenly denied the theological premises she was so adept at defending and agreed to Arminian tenets so that her boyfriend would marry her. I was seriously troubled by her cave-in, and I told her so. Now I was being asked to do the same thing.

I told him point-blank that I had thought through my position and that I would not simply check my brain at the door to be carried over the threshold. Nor would I lie. The matter was nonnegotiable. He backed down, and I accepted his marriage proposal. When he was able to get my father alone the following evening to ask his permission, Dad told him that I make my own decisions and he wouldn't commit himself. Mom, overhearing the conversation, had no hesitation about butting right in and denying her approval that hadn't been asked for. Her final words were, "You're trying to change her. We like Ruthie the way she is." I had not revealed my misgivings to her, but I'll never forget that warning.

Although he backed down by not making our getting married contingent on my belief in a six-day creation, he did insist (and I agreed) that I would read *The Genesis Flood* by Henry Morris and John Whitcomb. So convinced was he by the book's arguments that he was certain I would change my mind, though he assured me that once I read the book, I was free to come to my own conclusions. I carried out my end of the bargain and read the book, but I found it unconvincing. Throughout our marriage, I simply wanted the matter dropped. He refused. Time and again, he tried to compel me, sometimes violently, to accept his "science" of six days. *Black-and-white Bible, black-and-blue wife.*

During our engagement, I discovered just how different our families were. I grew up in a farm family with four siblings. He was an only child, growing up in sight of New York City. If my mother rattled him by strongly opposing our planned marriage, his mother rattled me even more. She was demanding and critical from the moment I met her. Among other things, she insisted I wear her ornate, ivory-colored wedding gown, which would require major alterations. I told her I had a style in mind and that I was really looking forward to shopping for my own dress. She was upset and made the dress an issue the entire week of my visit.

I had already learned from my fiancé that he had been expelled from Wheaton College for cheating and for breaking into a faculty office in search of exam answers. Two years later, he had been forced to leave Miami Christian College for behavior he did not clearly explain. And he was arrested as a peeping Tom near his parents' home on Long Island. All this, he had told me, had been cured through counseling. Knowing he had sought and been denied readmission to Wheaton, I was taken aback when his mother insisted that our marriage be held in a compromise location between my family's home and hers—specifically in Wheaton at the college chapel. Wheaton? Unbelievably, this was not some sort of sick joke.

The marriage plans went forward, but the Schroon Lake paradise had lost its magic. How many weeks or months, I sometimes wonder, did Eve gaze at her perfect lover before her eyes were opened? I am her child; we are all her children. And through the centuries, we, too, have been forever building Edens.

We are the centuries . . .
We march in spite of Hell, we do—Atrophy,
Entropy, and Proteus vulgaris, telling bawdy
jokes about a farm girl name of Eve and
a traveling salesman called Lucifer.

We bury your dead and their reputations.
We bury you. We are the centuries.
Be born then, gasp wind, screech at the surgeon's
slap, seek manhood, taste a little godhood, feel
pain, give birth, struggle a little while, succumb:
(Dying, leave quietly by the rear exit, please.)
Generation, regeneration, again, again, as in a
ritual, with blood-stained vestments and nail-
torn hands, children of Merlin, chasing a gleam.
Children, too, of Eve, forever building Edens . . .[6]

3

mutuality in living color

Fashioning a Marriage Based on Equality

A good marriage is like a kaleidoscope. With a few simple ingredients it is ever-changing, showing new facets of each other and the pleasure of working and living and loving as a team. A marriage can be whatever you want it to be . . . Your marriage is your very own; it belongs to no one else. If you try to live out someone else's idea of marriage, you may . . . get a pattern that does not fit at all. So it is important to realize that it is your marriage and that you can write your own rules.

PATRICIA GUNDRY, *HEIRS TOGETHER*

I love kaleidoscopes fashioned with multicolored glass shards. On more than one occasion, I have given beautifully designed Sheryl Koch kaleidoscopes as wedding gifts—all the better when they are accompanied by the above quote from *Heirs Together*, a volume I wished my husband would have been willing to work through with me back in the 1980s when I still had some optimism that our marriage could be saved.

The book, however, is ideally read before a couple even becomes engaged. It prepares a couple for the potential that this kaleidoscope may shatter. It alerts them to shards along the way—a signal to the engaged couple that they should step back and slow down and perhaps each take a different course.

Yet despite all the warning signs during our courtship, I foolishly believed ours would be a kaleidoscope marriage made in heaven.

Just before we tied the knot in August 1968, however, new issues came to the fore. On the day before the wedding, he demanded that we each memorize his personally contrived and lengthy, convoluted vows. I was shocked. He had earlier demanded that my promise to obey him must be in the vows. I agreed without fully considering the implications. But now he was asking for much more. What about *my* input and editing? There was no time, he insisted. What could I do? I was trapped, convinced it was too late to back out. I knew the little Alliance church (not the Wheaton College chapel) would be filled the following evening with family and neighborhood friends. Canceling would absolutely humiliate my mother.

I was a beautiful bride (with pictures to prove it!) in the simple white floor-length dress I had purchased on sale for $124. But the ceremony was marked by my stumbling through sentence after sentence, with repeated promptings by the poor preacher. The pieces of cut glass that I had hoped would form the intricate kaleidoscope of our life together had already begun to scatter. Here, first in the little church in Wisconsin; then in Montclair and Cape May Court House, New Jersey; later in Barrington Hills and Woodstock, Illinois; Crown

Point, Indiana; and finally in Grand Rapids, Michigan. Bloody shards wherever we lived—until nothing beautiful was left.

Little matters of authoritarian control had arisen on our honeymoon. A few days into the trip, we were passing through Montreal in the early afternoon. Our stash of packed snacks had been consumed. I spotted a sign for twenty-five-cent hot dogs. Our night's lodging had not provided breakfast, and I was *starving*. His plan was to find a smorgasbord dinner at around six o'clock, where we could eat enough to keep us fed until the following evening, something he did often. If it worked for him, it would work for me. So while Canada was passing outside our car windows, we were fussing and fighting. He prevailed. We did not stop for food. Nor, however, did I starve.

Perhaps what is most startling about my engagement story is that I was not entirely naive about life. On my own after high school, I applied for scholarships and worked my way through college and on into graduate school. I had owned vehicles and rented apartments. I was not seventeen and homeschooled. But whether the problem was serious gullibility or the serpent's lie that male headship was God's ideal, I stumbled into a very bad marriage.

When we revisit the Garden of Eden, we find that Eve has encountered the serpent, and she and Adam have taken the fall. God seeks them out in the cool of the evening. When charged with disobedience, Adam blames Eve, and Eve blames the serpent. Then come the curses. For Eve, the penalty is harsh—bearing children in pain and sorrow and, take note of this, gender inequality—the man ruling over her. There is no hint of such in the garden, but now, banished outside its walls, the mutuality she had enjoyed with Adam is absent.

Some Bible interpreters argue that this curse of inequality is prescriptive for all times—that we dare not tamper with it. But the curse on the ground that meant Adam would be tilling the soil snarled with thorns and thistles has been largely reversed. Even as inventions of machinery and fertilizers have relieved the backbreaking work of agriculture (at least in many areas of the world), so have legal statutes mitigated the effects of gender inequality.

The struggle for gender equality in civic life, as well as in church and in marriage, has been long and hard, and it is certainly not over. In the West today, women's equality in the political arena is assumed, though most people are unaware that a century ago, it was not. Women's equality in the church and in marriage, however, is still seriously restricted, particularly among conservative evangelicals.

When I first began digging in to the subject of biblical equality in the early 1980s, those who did not affirm gender equality were termed traditionalists. Indeed, they identified themselves as such and forthrightly argued that the Bible did not support women's equality in the church or in marriage. Today, the politically correct term *complementarian* is preferred, and along with it comes the claim that women are actually equal with men. They are denied positions of authority in the church and must be in subjection to their husbands, but they—as complementarians assert—enjoy equality all the same.

Imagine saying that African Americans are fully equal to whites before God, but they are not permitted to hold church office and must be subject to Caucasians. The claim would be ludicrous. And so it is regarding gender.

Yesterday, the day after Martin Luther King Jr. Day, 2015, John and I went to the theater to see *Selma*, the heart-wrenching story of the preparations for the march from Selma to Montgomery. Highest on the agenda during the repeated efforts to organize that 1965 peaceful march was voting rights. For that right, Jimmie Lee Jackson and others were killed. Many more, including longtime congressman John Lewis, were brutally beaten. They risked their lives for equality—equal rights in voting. Others earlier had risked their lives by merely going to church—in particular, the 16th Street Baptist Church in Birmingham. On September 16, 1963, four young girls were killed by a KKK bomb:

Addie Mae Collins
Cynthia Wesley
Carole Robertson
Denise McNair

The film brought back stark memories of the first months of my marriage. The first violent outburst occurred in October 1968, barely two months after our wedding. My ex-husband, to my surprise, announced that he was supporting George Wallace's independent run in the presidential race. He had been collecting literature and even attended a rally in Newark. I strongly opposed Wallace, though I mainly kept my thoughts to myself. Our differences erupted very suddenly one afternoon when I had returned to the apartment later than usual, surprised to find him still there. He asked where I'd been. I told him I'd gotten my absentee ballot in the mail, filled it out, and walked to the nearby mailbox to mail it. He asked me which candidate I voted for. I told him. He went into a rage, demanding why I hadn't voted for Wallace. My words only infuriated him further. When he pushed me, I recovered and stood my ground, almost daring him to lay a hand on his new bride. I reminded him that women had won the right to vote with the 19th Amendment in 1919—a right that did not mean a woman had to vote as her husband did. He angrily countered that my obedience to him was foremost.

The matter of my lack of submission simmered, as did his rage. I had defied him as "the head of the home" by not voting for the candidate I knew he supported. My refusal to support George Wallace had everything to do with his racist administration as governor of Alabama and his sending of officers to kill and beat peaceful marchers.

Until yesterday, I had not thought about Wallace in years. There he was on the big screen, mostly played by another but also in actual newsreel footage. True, he later apologized (after he was paralyzed in 1972 by a would-be assassin). But had he possessed moral scruples as a governor, he could have stopped the killings of innocent individuals. Instead he exercised his leadership in the state of Alabama with vicious power. Had he done what was moral and right, Addie, Cynthia, Carole, and Denise might today be cuddling grandchildren. Some of the decades-long racism so prevalent still today might have been stomped out. It was this man, I was reminded yesterday, I had refused to vote for.

Without equal rights there is no equality. To argue that male headship does not infringe on female equality is disingenuous. There is no definition of equality that does not at the same time grant *equal rights* and *opportunities*. If, on the other hand, complementarians were to argue that the Bible does not extend equal rights to women, that would not be disingenuous. In fact, as well versed as I am in the issues relating to the egalitarian and headship debate, I could make that very case myself. What I could not do is argue that the meaning of equality does not include equal rights and opportunity—that *inequality* in a marriage is actually *equality.*

Very early in my first marriage, the Ephesians 5 passage was frequently used against me, always in a one-sided manner. That my ex-husband failed to love me as Christ loved the church was not applicable. That I was not submitting to him was the overriding issue. Anyone familiar with this passage knows that it begins in verse 21: "Submit to one another out of reverence for Christ." The next phrase, "wives, to your own husbands," has no verb in the original Greek. It is a verse that cannot be read without the topic sentence of mutual submission. Moreover, the entire passage places a far heavier burden of love and submission on the husband than it does on the wife, as I have written elsewhere:

> It is safe to say that in the ancient world, Paul's admonition
> to women did not amount to shocking news. That a wife should
> submit to her husband was obvious. That was part of the very
> fabric of society and culture. But that husband and wife were to
> "be subject to one another" had to be rather startling. And that
> a husband was to "love his wife as Christ loved the church" was
> certainly a standard far beyond what was expected of husbands
> in the ancient world.

> If anyone squirmed in the pew of the first-century church,
> it surely must have been the husband, not the wife.[1]

Here Paul is speaking of mutuality as in 1 Corinthians 11:11–12: "Woman is not independent of man, nor is man independent of woman. For as woman came from man, so also man is born of woman. But everything comes from God."

An earlier passage in Paul's first letter to the church at Corinth, frequently employed to bolster male headship, also supports equality in marriage. Here Paul starts by pointing out the benefits of celibacy and the immorality of adulterous relationships, clearly making the latter an *equal* prohibition. He continues with this advice for marital balance and mutuality:

> The husband should fulfill his marital duty to his wife, and likewise the wife to her husband. The wife does not have authority over her own body but yields it to her husband. In the same way, the husband does not have authority over his own body but yields it to his wife. Do not deprive each other except perhaps by mutual consent and for a time, so that you may devote yourselves to prayer. Then come together again so that Satan will not tempt you because of your lack of self-control.
>
> 1 CORINTHIANS 7:3–5

Mutual consent. Here Paul is dealing with ministry matters. He is a driven man—driven to preach the gospel—and he wants others to do likewise. Such activity is easily undermined when encumbered by a spouse and children. So he privileges singleness, something rarely promoted by complementarians today. When men and women do marry, however, *mutual consent* is the principle, and we are unnecessarily narrowing his focus if we apply the phrase to sexual intercourse alone. Mutual consent in any aspect of day-to-day intercourse between a husband and wife simply makes sense. If, on the other hand, Paul is admonishing the husband to be ruler over his wife, why does he not insist that he rule over sexual intimacies as well?

Referring to complementarian marriages that demonstrate male headship, Russell Moore writes, "Sometimes I fear that we have marriages that are functionally egalitarian."[2] If such marriages are not supposed to be functionally egalitarian, how are they supposed to work out? How do patriarchal marriages work out in practical terms? Years ago, I asked a colleague at Trinity to help explain how headship played out on a daily basis. He told me his family had just returned from Miami, Ohio, where his son visited a university. As they considered where to eat along the way, the others in the car expressed their preference for Taco Bell. He exercised his headship and chose a different fast-food restaurant. And thus he ruled. But what if the wife questions his decision. Here John Piper has provided a script:

> Suppose it's Noël and I. I am about to decide something for the family that looks foolish to her. At that moment, Noël could express her submission like this: "Johnny [who knew?], I know you've thought a lot about this, and I love it when you take the initiative to plan for us and take the responsibility like this, but I really don't have peace about this decision and I think we need to talk about it some more. Could we? Maybe tonight sometime?"[3]

Why must a wife respond in such a way? Piper states elsewhere, "A wife who 'comes on strong' with her advice will probably drive a husband into passive silence or into active anger."[4] While he is no doubt explaining—not excusing—wife battering, the term "active anger" brings back a lot of memories of violence, and not always directed entirely at me. I know from experience that active anger can rip cabinet doors right off their hinges, a phone off the wall, and put a dent in a refrigerator door all in one episode, not to mention bloody knuckles and a blood-spattered floor. That I was cowering and pleading for him to stop had little effect on his "active anger."

Bruce Ware, who years ago was a colleague of mine at Trinity, stated the matter even more forcefully at a 2008 conference when he said that "women victims of domestic violence were often to blame for their own abuse because they were failing to submit to their husbands' authority."[5]

Blaming the woman will be dealt with in a later chapter. Here the issue is practical insights on the workings of complementarian and egalitarian marriages. How do egalitarians work out differences in their marriages? Who is the tiebreaker? When I had asked my complementarian colleague about how his headship might look in relationship to the daily routine, I had actually expected something more significant than whether or not to eat at Taco Bell. As much as they may tout headship, most complementarian husbands do not want to be saddled with all the decision making.

This is certainly true for egalitarians. How do egalitarians deal with a tiebreaker situation? Let's say the husband is offered a transfer with a substantial salary increase; the wife is settled in the neighborhood—near family, schools, and church. But the husband wants the opportunity to climb the career ladder. Or let's say the situation is reversed, and the wife has an opportunity to climb the ladder to success. Such a life-changing decision should simply be based on mutuality, and no major move should be made until both husband and wife are fully on board. Can this lead to serious conflict? Of course it can, no matter whether the marriage is based on equality or on male headship.

It is interesting that the concept of male headship and wifely submission is rarely even broached in the Hebrew Bible. The longest passage in the Bible that deals with marriage features the wife. She is the Proverbs 31 superwoman who is more precious than rubies. But there is no hint of her being anything less than a full equal of any man around—including her husband, who "has full confidence in her" (verse 11). She is not waiting for him to make decisions and serve as tiebreaker. Rather, we find her busy with her cottage garment industry, selling items throughout the region, and not only that, but also dealing in real estate and planting a vineyard. She serves her husband and children as well, but the text shows her first and foremost to be a shrewd businesswoman, clothed with strength, dignity, wisdom, and laughter—a woman who opens her arms to the poor.

In the Gospels, we find Mary, mother of Jesus, in a nearly parallel role. If we were to travel with her, we might find it difficult to keep up. Priscilla is another wife who has a cottage industry (tentmaking) and travels in ministry, working alongside her husband, Aquila, and the apostle Paul.

When we move beyond the first century to the time when the church is beginning to become more organized, however, crucial restrictions are often placed on wives. "If the more important, most beneficial concerns were turned over to the woman, she would go quite mad," wrote John Chrysostom. "God maintained the order of each sex by dividing the business of human life into two parts and assigned the more necessary and beneficial aspects to the man and the less important, inferior matters to the woman."[6] He emphasizes that this is not simply a societal measure, but a plan given by God "so that a woman would not rebel against the husband due to the inferiority of her service."[7] Tell that to those confident and capable biblical women.

Read and reread Proverbs 31, and it's hard to imagine how one would find this woman to be "quite mad." She is involved in both the "more necessary and beneficial" work as well as the "less important, inferior matters" (assuming—as I surely do not—that home, family, and charitable causes are "inferior"). Chrysostom was interpreting Scripture with a male bias—a bias that has been almost universally passed along and accepted from his time to the present day. The vast majority of Bible interpreters, after all, have been male.

A marriage based on mutuality offers many benefits that are not, at least in theory, applicable to a marriage based on male headship. Consider the matter of Alzheimer's disease. What if Robertson McQuilkin, instead of Muriel, had been stricken. She would have had to, for all practical purposes, assume *headship*. A marriage of mutuality would have better prepared her for that. Consider widowhood. Would the Proverbs 31 woman have been prepared to manage the household without her husband? Of course she would have. Is a woman who is ruled by her husband prepared? When a husband makes the decisions, a wife is left in a vulnerable position upon his death.

Catherine Marshall married Peter Marshall when she was a junior in college. The following year, he was called to be the minister of the prestigious New York Avenue Presbyterian Church in Washington, D.C. Several years later, he was appointed as chaplain of the United States Senate. He was handsome, charming, brilliant, and articulate, frequently asked to speak at important functions out of town. He lived out the doctrine of male headship in marriage, and Catherine remained in the background. In January 1949, he took part in the inauguration ceremony of President Harry Truman. Five days later, he was dead.

The heart attack that took her husband's life took the wind out of Catherine. She was bowed down in grief. But there was more. I wrote of her situation in *Private Lives of Pastors' Wives*:

> As the weeks wore on, Catherine quickly discovered that there was more than grief to cope with. Few women could have been less prepared for independence than she. "In many ways, I was still a little girl. I had adored and leaned on my husband . . . I had never once figured out an income tax blank, had a car inspected, consulted a lawyer, or tried to read an insurance policy." These were not the kinds of things that Peter believed ought to concern a housewife. To complicate matters, Peter had not left a will, which meant that, according to District of Columbia statutes, two-thirds of the estate would be placed in trust for young Peter, and Catherine would receive only a third. Even her son's guardianship had to be established in court.[8]

In 1950, when Catherine was struggling to find her way, male headship was assumed. Only in recent decades, however, has male headship been politicized. An example of this can be found in the recent changes made in the Southern Baptist Convention (SBC), the largest Protestant denomination in America. I am personally aware of the pain these changes caused many women through conversations I've had with the late Dellanna West O'Brien, onetime director of the Woman's Missionary Union (WMU). In 1993, Adrian Rogers (three-time president of the SBC) proclaimed that the WMU must be "hardwired" to the SBC instead of continuing on in its supportive, though independent role. When the leadership of the WMU balked, they were likened to an adulterous woman.

Only a few years later, in 1998, the SBC, meeting in Salt Lake City, made a public pronouncement on women in the denomination, under the banner of the Family Amendment. Newspapers around the country carried this new directive. From *The New York Times:*

> [The Convention] amended its essential statement of beliefs today to include a declaration that a woman should "submit herself graciously" to her husband's leadership and that a husband should "provide for, protect and lead his family" . . . Paige Patterson, a seminary president from North Carolina who was elected today as the Southern Baptists' president, said the amendment was a response to "a time of growing crisis in the family."[9]

A crisis in the family that Paige Patterson did not note, nor did the Family Amendment reference, was (and is) domestic violence. That the SBC added the Family Amendment might be regarded as a relatively harmless measure. But it was devastating for certain long-time SBC missionaries who were recalled from their posts because they refused to sign on to the new statement of faith.

One of the results of the SBC's clampdown on the WMU is that the once very significant role that single women missionaries played has since plummeted. How strange that is in light of the apostle Paul's emphasis on the ministry of single missionaries. Women like Lottie Moon, once regarded as the "patron saint" of Southern Baptist missions, would today not recognize their onetime denominational home. Indeed, the "Lottie Moon Christmas Offering" has over the decades brought in more money to missions than any other fund. She was an outspoken woman who proclaimed, "What women want who come to China is free opportunity to do the largest possible work . . . What women have a right to demand is perfect equality."[10]

She was an intelligent, independent thinker who is remembered for remarkable accomplishments—a model for all women. She was not held back by a John Chrysostom or by a Paige Patterson or by a husband demanding that his wife submit to his headship. Today the Lottie Moons of a century ago have all but disappeared in the SBC—a truly sad turn of events.

It is also a sad story when a confident and capable woman marries, only to be stripped of her most compelling qualities. Yet the doctrine of male headship demands that an independent single woman turn into another woman—a woman who is under subjection. Reflecting on his marriage to Patricia, Stan Gundry's words are well worth pondering.

> *I would not have been attracted to Pat in the first place had I not seen in her one who was my equal . . . But within a few days of marriage that began to change. Traditional ideas of male leadership and female submissiveness began to take over. It was so ingrained in us that at the time I don't think we really understood what was happening . . . After all too long a time, some years back we began to try to rediscover that original relationship . . . Living as equals has given me back the woman I was originally attracted to. It has brought us back to the basis for the relationship that we originally had.*[11]

4

abuse of power

Perversions in the Name of Patriarchy

While patriarchy may not be the overarching cause of all abuse, it is an enormously significant factor, because in traditional patriarchy, males have a disproportionate share of power . . . So while patriarchy is not the sole explanation for violence against women, we would expect that male headship would be distorted by insecure, unhealthy men to justify their domination and abuse of women.

STEVEN TRACY

One might imagine that the "insecure, unhealthy men" Steven Tracy refers to in this chapter's epigraph would be easily identified. We should be able to spot that sort of person—a staff member or a deacon at a church, the friendly neighbor next door. Most of the time, however, such men operate under the radar. My ex-husband was intelligent, articulate, and charming. Telltale signs of trouble were always blamed on others. In 1970, we moved from New Jersey, where we had lived for the first two years of our marriage, to the Chicago area, where he had been accepted for graduate studies at Trinity Evangelical Divinity School. Although his previous problems at other schools would not have been erased from the record, his high Graduate Record Exam scores were impressive enough for admission. Within a year, however, there were problems. His thesis director, upset by his obstinate attitude, refused to continue working with him, forcing him to find another professor, who agreed to take him on only if he wrote on an entirely different topic. He blamed his difficulties on "liberalism," on the school in general, and on both professors, though in the end, he completed a satisfactory thesis and was allowed to graduate.

With graduation in sight (now four years into our marriage), he applied to be a pastoral candidate of a small Bible church in Woodstock, Illinois. Of five candidates, the church chose him. In the three years that followed, I recall only one sermon that church elders found objectionable. On his first Mothers' Day in the pulpit, he preached on Mary, whom he verbally pummeled for trying to keep Jesus "tied to her apron strings." Say what? It was a thinly disguised rant against mothers and women in general. I sat in the congregation as bewildered as everyone else.

Yet attendance continued to increase to the point where new facilities were needed. Land was purchased, and my ex-husband prepared for the groundbreaking ceremony. Within months, however, in the spring of 1975, it was learned that he had been arrested for repeated theft of coffee and donut money at the county jail, where he had gone weekly to make pastoral visits.

The wretched shame I felt after we both had been confronted in our home by a church elder and his wife (who along with others—though not me—had seen the notice of the arrest in the local paper) was one of the most painful episodes of my marriage. I would have endured a dozen beatings to have escaped such humiliation. To my bewilderment, though, my ex-husband barely seemed bothered. To alleviate my sting of guilt, he agreed (on my insistence) to preach the following Sunday night a sermon of deep contrition from Psalm 51—a sermon I practically dictated to him.

As a result of his "sincere" and public apology, the church board allowed him to stay on until the end of the summer, giving us time to sell our house and for him to find another position. A number of people left the church, or at least temporarily stopped attending, but others treated us kindly, me in particular, mother of a toddler. On our last Sunday, some newer members, unaware of the behind-the-scenes negotiations, wept openly and seemed to blame the church leaders for the loss of their beloved pastor.

Despite a lengthy record of wrongdoing dating back to his early years at Wheaton College, his charm and obvious capabilities (and my behind-the-scenes maneuvering) opened doors for a Bible church ministry in Crown Point, Indiana, and further graduate studies at Grace Theological Seminary in Winona Lake, Indiana. I was very upset by what had happened in Woodstock (and questioned his claim to have been unfairly treated at Trinity), but he was my husband, and I was convinced that his commitment to turn his life around was for real. While new doors were opening, however, the violence behind closed doors continued. That was not how it was supposed to be. My dreams of a happy marriage continued to fade.

I've sometimes wondered about the wives of the biblical patriarchs. Did they, too, lose the hope of happiness? In my book *Dynamic Women of the Bible*, I have compared myself to a little-known patriarchal wife:

> I once lived on 532 Pleasant Street in a small Midwestern town surrounded by rich farmland and large dairy herds. It was an idyllic setting, or so it seemed on the surface. But sin and scandal were all too real. I was a young minister's wife and a new mother. Life was good. Then there was that unforgettable knock on the door. My world fell apart. We were forced to leave town unexpectedly and under a cloud as a result of the exposure of my husband's

hidden misdeeds. God might have rained down fire on that town or on us, but he did not. When we left, I looked back with anguish and guilt and utter sadness. Yes, I looked back. For me the shame was searing, and I can still feel that hot metaphorical sulfur singeing my skin now nearly forty years later.[1]

The allusion here is to Lot's wife. In certain ways, I identify with her. Sodom, like Woodstock, was a small town surrounded by farmland. Like me, she was no doubt a busy wife and mother who may have enjoyed gardening and hanging clothes on the line. We both fled town with our small families, and we both looked back. For me, there was no pillar of salt, only shame and sorrow.

Part of biblical patriarchy is passing the mantel on to the oldest son to carry on the generational line. But God has a way of turning things upside down, and we see time and again that the oldest son does not carry on the line, as was true with the sons of the three patriarchs—Abraham, Isaac, and Jacob. Patriarchs dominated their households as ruler of the family. Period. Except for the exceptions. We find that Sarah not only orders Abraham around, as in telling him to give her a baby through her maidservant Hagar, but we also find God telling Abraham to do what Sarah tells him to do when Sarah later orders Hagar out of the household.

As was true with the reversal of the old patriarchal practice of favoring the oldest son, so was it true that women sometimes ruled the roost. This is particularly the case with Rebekah. Through her clever manipulation, she managed to secure the blessing for her favorite second-born son, Jacob. Indeed, her manipulation and dishonesty rivaled that of her father-in-law, Abraham, who convinced the Egyptian pharaoh that Sarah was not his wife, but only his sister. Rachel, Jacob's favorite wife, was as devious as he was, sneaky enough to surreptitiously steal her father's household gods and then lie about it.

The Bible is a gold mine for anyone seeking to understand domestic relationships, and it spares nothing by way of family dysfunction. Whole books have been written on these patriarchs who walk out of the pages of Genesis, and we could write a treatise on just their domestic relationships alone. But for the purpose of this volume, it is important to understand how abuse, even domestic violence, is passed down from generation to generation. It is also significant to recognize that even as Abraham's sin of betraying Sarah is not censured by God, neither is Rebekah's pattern of manipulation. More significantly, Rebekah is not censured by God for taking on what would have been considered her husband's rightful patriarchal duties.

The wives of Old Testament patriarchs do not live enviable lives. They are expected to give birth to sons, and for the three most-noted of them—Sarah, Rebekah, and Rachel—it becomes a painful struggle. Indeed, this is another pattern that emerges in the Genesis account. Sarah's ordeal is familiar—that of giving birth to her only child at age ninety. Rebekah, who bears twins, endures twenty years of barrenness prior to that most painful childbirth. Rachel is initially barren and competes with the fertile Leah for babies until finally giving birth to Joseph and Benjamin.

Although the patriarchs in Genesis are not known as good husbands and fathers, there are men in the Old Testament who are admirable. Elkanah, married to Hannah, is a loving husband who is anguished by her barrenness. His words are those of a compassionate husband desperately seeking to bring comfort: "Hannah, why are you weeping? Why don't you eat? Why are you downhearted? Don't I mean more to you than ten sons?" (1 Samuel 1:8). Here in this ancient patriarchal age is a man who deeply loves his wife—and not just because she's giving him sons (since he has another wife for whom baby making is her forte). He's touched by her heartbreak. Later she has the joy of bearing children, and her firstborn, Samuel, grows up to be a fine man and, for my money, the greatest prophet in Israel.

Another example of a caring patriarch is Boaz, who comes to life in the story of Naomi and Ruth. "Introduced into the narrative as a man of valor," writes Carolyn Custis James, he "has a lot to lose. Yet amazingly, even with two strong women in his life . . . Boaz gains significantly. He . . . is not diminished, marginalized, or feminized in the slightest by being outnumbered and influenced by Ruth and Naomi."[2]

Indeed, one of the most intriguing marriages in the Old Testament is arranged by Naomi, who sends her widowed daughter-in-law in the dark of night to, some say, seduce an older man with deep pockets. Naomi clearly lays out her purpose:

> "My daughter, I must find a home for you, where you will be well provided for . . . Tonight he will be winnowing barley on the threshing floor. Wash, put on perfume, and get dressed in your best clothes . . . When he lies down, note the place where he is lying. Then go and uncover his feet and lie down. He will tell you what to do."
>
> RUTH 3:1–4

The plan works. Soon Ruth and Boaz have a bouncing baby boy, Obed. The text tells us how elated grandmother Naomi is, though we doubt her joy exceeds that of Boaz, who has become the father of the most beautiful little baby boy in Bethlehem—a boy who will grow up to be the father of Jesse and grandfather of David.

Though David is the darling of the ladies—and the Lord—he does not treat women well. Indeed, he treated his first wife, Michal (daughter of King Saul), badly. To him, she was no more than a royal trophy. Yet she loved David and loyally protected him when her father was seeking to kill him. But soon, Saul demanded that she be sent away from David and married to another man, Paltiel. We know little about this man except that he was devoted to his wife. After Saul died, David commanded that his royal trophy be returned to him, though surely not for love. Here are some of the saddest lines in Scripture: "Then David sent . . . orders and had [Michal] taken away from her husband Paltiel son of Laish. Her husband, however, went with her, weeping behind her all the way to Bahurim. Then Abner said to him, 'Go back home!' So he went back" (2 Samuel 3:14–16).

As we read of these generations in Genesis and beyond, it is also important to consider our own ancestry and how it may have been infected by generations of dysfunction and domestic violence. The only family patriarch I knew well when I was growing up was my mother's father. He was a nice old man who gave us each a dollar on our birthdays. Then one evening, everything changed. I was thirteen and had taken over my older brother's chores of milking the cows. I was alone and greeted him as he came through the barn door. I went about my work and may have been kidding with him as usual when all of a sudden he grabbed me and kissed me hard on the lips. Horrified, I pulled away and immediately got back to my work.

Later, after he had left, I told my mother in no uncertain terms that if Grandpa ever came to the barn again while I was there, I would walk off the job. What is most stunning about this encounter, as I later reflected, was that my mother's only comment was that she would make sure he would never again go to the barn while I was there. And she did. I remember her coming out as soon as he drove his truck into the yard. She would take a position between him and the barn. She kept him at bay. But why didn't she question me further? Had she herself been abused? Discussing that episode after she had died, my two sisters and I surmised that she may have been abused by her father, particularly after we learned that he had for years sexually abused a cousin. And we also learned about another "wife" (and children he sired) who lived on the Iron Range in Minnesota. He spent more time there than was required for a second job.

Grandpa died many years ago. How am I supposed to remember him? As an evil man only? He is part of my heritage, my bloodline. Far more distant on my father's side is Helmut Stellrecht, a strategist for Adolf Hitler now rating his own German language Wikipedia entry. How do we deal with ancestries sullied and corrupted by every kind of cruelty? Is it our duty to own that heritage and vow to do what we can to turn it around? It was my good fortune to have parents who did not perpetuate abuse. But my marriage to an abuser set the stage for such behavior to be passed on to future generations.

We see this same pattern among the patriarchs and those who followed them. But *patriarch* does not necessarily carry with it negative connotations. He is the male head of the family (as opposed to matriarch), and when given that, the connotation is a respected and wise man. Although patriarchy has gotten a bad press, a respected wise grandfather or father or husband who has a reputation for fatherliness and strength of character is a key ingredient in turning a pattern of abuse around.

This concept of patriarchy is appealing to many women, particularly in the black community, where fatherhood is too often a missing element. There is, according to the late Don Browning, who was a leading scholar on marriage, an alarming "world fatherhood problem."[3] More serious than authoritarian headship is male "neglect, absence and failure of responsibility."[4]

When comparing equality in marriage to racial equality, as I have previously done, it is only fair to say that many African-American women might not see the same parallel. Like white women, they certainly confront domestic violence perpetrated by husbands and fathers of their children. So, even while asserting their equal place in the marriage, the most important issue to them is a caring man who is responsible, present, and accounted for.

And so it was for me. That my ex-husband was violent toward me (and occasionally toward Carlton) is only part of the picture. That he later entirely abandoned his patriarchal role as father, leaving a thirteen-year-old boy floundering, is one more example of the "world fatherhood problem." It is a sad reality among whites as well as blacks. For nearly twenty years, Carlton did not know where his father lived and had no means of contacting him—until a cousin located him through his online search capabilities. When Carlton later surprised his father with a visit to his home on St. Simons Island, the conversation was awkward. Sure, they could pet the dogs and laugh at their playfulness, but then what? It would have been too revealing for his father to ask, Did you ever finish eighth grade? Graduate from high school? Play any sports? Get married? (The answer to that question was perhaps assumed, since Carlton was accompanied by his thirteen-year-old daughter.)

Where was his father for those momentous events? He would have had no trouble finding Carlton, whose address remained the same for many years. Absent father at sports meets. Absent father at graduation. Absent father at wedding. Absent father who never heard a granddaughter's baby talk, who never read her a picture book or heard her sing a solo with the Girls Choral Academy. Failed patriarchy. A sad, drawn-out episode in the world fatherhood problem. In recent years, Carlton has on many occasions introduced me and John as "my mom and dad." Carlton and John get along very well and have an easy father/son relationship—John's only son, Carlton's only dad.

The Bible offers powerful pictures of patriarchy, both good and bad. The story of the prodigal son is a classic. Here Jesus is talking about God and his love for his children—in this case, a son who wastes his inheritance and is utterly wasted himself. But the Father's strong arms embrace the son and welcome him home. What a beautiful picture of patriarchy!

Patriarchy as it is perceived today is often very different from Old Testament patriarchy. In fact, the Christian Patriarchy movement in North America has moved into reality TV with the Duggar family. "Though the Duggars do describe themselves as conservative Christians," writes Kathryn Joyce, "in reality, they follow a . . . pro-life-purist lifestyle known as Quiverfull, where women forgo all birth-control options . . . This resurgent emphasis on women's submissiveness takes many forms,"[5] including the Southern Baptist statement that the wife must "graciously submit" to her husband's "loving headship" (as well as the many books published by the Council on Biblical Manhood and Womanhood).

If not offspring of the same parents, these parachurch movements—Quiverfull, the Patriarchy movement, and the Council on Biblical Manhood and Womanhood (CBMW)—are kissing cousins. All three strongly promote male headship and female submission and marriage at a young age that produces many offspring. In fact, an article posted on the CBMW website by assistant editor Greg Gibson is titled, "5 Reasons Why Getting Married Young Is Still a Good Thing." Here he states his underlying thesis clearly: "When you as a young person embrace the pursuit of early marriage, you are standing firm on the Word of God by embracing the roles God has designed for you at an early age. By doing this, you are reflecting back to the world, not only God's design for gender roles, but also God's design for marriage."[6]

The CBMW's promotion of young marriage is closely related to the concept of "dateship" promoted by Owen Strachan, executive director of the organization. Dateship is dependent on a patriarchal father—or father figure—who determines if an initial meeting for coffee can be permitted to progress to the next level. The steps for continuing are summed up in a guest blog by Tim Fall on *The Wartburg Watch 2015*:

- First date goes well? The man asks the father for a second date with his daughter.
- Next step goes well? The man asks the father for permission to court his daughter.
- That step goes well? The man asks the father for permission to marry his daughter.

While those in CBMW and in the Patriarchy and Quiverfull movements regard these steps as proper for courting and dateship, in reality, there are many absent fathers and fathers like my own, who wasn't willing to play that role, even if I had wanted him to. Nor does Strachan's proposal work for many couples, each living on their own, who are contemplating marriage, as Tim Fall's scenario humorously suggests:

> "Sir, your daughter and I had coffee together and now I'd like to take her to dinner."

"What do you do for a living?"

"I'm CEO of a Fortune 500 company."

"All right, you can take her out this weekend. I'll tell her to cancel her trip to Europe as head of the U.S. delegation to the economic summit."[7]

In its introduction to Tim Fall's guest blog, *The Wartburg Watch* also makes reference to the child marriage of Maranatha, daughter of Stan Owen, who was a "spiritual mentor" to Matthew Chapman, a ministerial student at Baylor University. Matthew expressed his interest in Maranatha when she was thirteen. They began living together as a married couple (having essentially gone through the process of dateship) when she was fifteen and he was twenty-eight, a union that took place in the 1990s and has received widespread publicity on the Internet. Did the marriage work out? Apparently so. In 2008, the couple's daughter, Lauren, shortly after her sixteenth birthday, married a twenty-six-year-old man.[8]

There are many red flags regarding this Patriarchy movement, particularly as it is utilized to prop up a species of male headship that often borders on abuse and sometimes clearly goes over the line. "Wife spanking," as absurd as it sounds, is defended among those on the fringe of the Patriarchy movement. I once knew a woman who told me she had been spanked on a number of occasions early in her marriage by a very decent man I highly respected in every other way. He is now deceased, and I've lost contact with his wife, but I think back and wonder, How could that have been true? And I also wonder why I wasn't shocked by her story. "Lauren" (not the Lauren above), who writes anonymously, presents in detail a sobering version of her story:

> My husband was only two years older (but he is close to 6 feet tall and heavily muscled and I am around 5 feet tall and under 100 pounds) . . . Calling it just a "spanking" in some ways covers up what is going on, I think. I know for a long time I did not consider myself a battered or abused wife . . . It ranged anywhere from a swat or two over my clothing up to him pulling

down my pants for episodes that left me bawling. But he never swore, or acted out of control. So I deluded myself to thinking that I wasn't like those women in shelters scared for their lives . . . My wedding vows included a vow to obey and he would often remind me that God commanded wives to submit and obey their husbands as they were supposed to do toward Christ. The thing is I never felt "threatened." Just utterly powerless.[9]

Where, if any, is there common ground among those who call for equality in marriage and those who argue for male headship? Russell Moore, who heads up the Ethics Commission for the Southern Baptist Convention, has chided fellow complementarians for their lack of enthusiasm for the terms *patriarchal* and *patriarchy*. He rightly points out that complementarians are playing into contemporary culture rather than being countercultural: "Even to use the word 'patriarchy' in an evangelical context is uncomfortable since the word is deemed 'negative' even by most complementarians. But evangelicals should ask why patriarchy seems negative to those of us who serve the God of Abraham, Isaac, and Jacob—the God *and Father* of Jesus Christ."[10]

There is much in Moore's overall perspective on male headship with which I disagree, but there is also common ground. Patriarchy is certainly an honest way for proponents of male headship to identify themselves, and strong and wise fatherhood is critical for healthy families. In a good marriage where there are children, strength and wisdom characterize both parents. How I wished that my ex-husband had been such a father and that I could look back to my grandfather as the great patriarch of the family.

It is unfortunate that so many Christians today who tout family values and strong father figures at the same time curtail women's roles. Indeed unfortunate, when we realize that mutuality in marriage offers the securest foundation for a family. I resonate with the words of Carolyn Osiek:

*I fully support the renewal of fatherhood
and fatherly responsibility.
I do not believe that it must be at
the expense of women.*[11]

5

what if women ruled the world?

Celebrating Gender Differences

What if, instead of three wise men . . .

Three wise women would have . . .
asked directions, arrived on time,
helped deliver the baby, cleaned the
stable, made a casserole, and brought
practical gifts.

What if women ruled the world? I once posed this hypothetical question in my course on leadership at Calvin Theological
Seminary. Then I asked the students to imagine what the seminary
would be like if all the school's presidents, top administrators, and
faculty had been women for some 130 years. The reverse had actually been true, except for me. The students, including the one woman
in the class, seemed perplexed. Why would I even ask such a question? What was my point? Besides the fact that I love to contemplate
counterfactuals, I wanted my students to think seriously about gender

differences between men and women. So, *what if* women ruled the world? Seminaries and institutions of all kinds, including the institution of marriage, would be very different if women were in charge—or even if they enjoyed full equality.

For a time in the 1960s and beyond, some feminists and others believed that, apart from anatomy, male and female were essentially the same. I emphasize *some* because many early feminists looked to Germaine Greer for understanding. An Australian, she was the author of *The Female Eunuch* (1970), an international bestseller. Greer was a controversial figure, even among feminists of her day.

The Wikipedia entry on Germaine Greer reads as follows:

> Greer is a liberation rather than equality feminist. Her goal is not equality with men, which she sees as assimilation and settling to live the lives of "unfree men" . . . She argues that women's liberation means embracing sex differences in a positive fashion—a struggle for the freedom of women to "define their own values, order their own priorities, and decide their own fate."[1]

Egalitarians do not deny the significance of gender differences. Indeed, such differences are not easily dismissed. Today almost everyone realizes you can't just hand a girl a truck and a boy a doll and bend their gender proclivities.

I have one child—a son. I once tried the doll experiment, though not on him. Even if I had wanted Carlton to play with dolls, it would have been a futile effort. But my brother Jonnie, I believed, was a good candidate. He was six; I was eight. We climbed trees together, so why not play dolls? With no male ego to protect, he was in. I had a sizable collection, so I gave him Annie. We would take journeys together through the fields and woods with an old baby buggy filled with dolls. The only problem was his treatment of Annie, whom he promptly undressed and renamed Rubber-noggin. When we approached the pond, he would run ahead and hurl her into the water to see how fast she could swim. He flung her at gophers and birds and fence posts.

When her head came off, it bothered him not in the least. He loved to play with Annie. So much for my experiment.

Major clinical studies, with many more subjects and far greater analysis than I gave my own experiment, have reinforced the premise that gender differences cannot be accounted for by nurture alone. One study confirmed that the differences stem from different regions of the brain. This widely publicized research released by the University of Basel in January 2015 suggests that "women generally experience higher levels of emotional stimulation than men." More than three thousand subjects were tested by showing them negative and positive images. Women "rated these images as more emotionally stimulating than men." This rating exercise was followed by a memory test that was also telling:

> The female participants were able to recall significantly more of the images than their male counterparts. The women had a particularly enhanced ability to recall the positive images. The study's lead author, Dr. Annette Milnik, explained, "This would suggest that gender-dependent differences in emotional processing and memory are due to different mechanisms."[2]

Such studies have enormous significance for women in marriage and in the church. Indeed, I have always argued that gender difference bolsters the need for gender equality. Whether in the United States Senate, corporate industry, higher education, or religion, we need to hear the voices and consider the decision making of women. Women bring different issues and understandings to the table. The same is true in marriage. A family and a marriage are weakened when the husband dominates and his decisions are the only valid ones. On the other hand, when children see their parents operating under the banner of an equal partnership and at the same time expressing gender differences, both girls and boys move more naturally through a healthy adolescence and into adulthood.

Gender is identity. More than anything else, we are either male or female. The first words spoken at the birth of any child are "it's a girl" or "it's a boy." The immediate physical difference that expands in the ensuing years, combined with hormonal, emotional, and other differences, has a profound impact on every aspect of life, including domestic violence. Any problem has the potential of being met with physical force, powered by hormones and lack of empathy. If the problem itself relates to the topic of gender, any spark is capable of detonating an explosion.

The setting was our dining room. I had flown into Grand Rapids from Chicago, having finished an intensive two days of teaching at Trinity. My ex-husband picked me up at the airport. I could tell he was in a foul mood. Before we arrived home, he raised the topic of the women elders elected the previous evening at our church's annual congregational meeting. They would be the first-ever female elders at Fifth Reformed Church in 1985, one hundred years after it was founded. Amid my hectic schedule, I had forgotten about this critical meeting.

Although I had not voted, his anger was directed at me. After we arrived home, he demanded that I verbally stand with him against women in office. When I refused and remained silent, he began pummeling me, pushing me, knocking me to the floor, and kicking me. As I had done before, I went into self-defense mode. I curled into a fetal position, my arms, legs, and head tightly tucked. He stopped kicking. It was over. He walked away. *Black-and-white Bible, black-and-blue wife.*

I later learned from our pastor that during that congregational meeting, my ex-husband had gotten up, without any warning, and distributed and read a written statement on why women should be prohibited from office. If there were some in the congregation who were undecided, his conduct that night may have had an opposite effect from the one he intended.

Several months later, a male elder commented to me how the consistory had changed since women had joined the group. These two homemakers, whose children were grown, were actively involved in a variety of local ministries. Their presence often redirected discussion toward personal and family issues in the congregation and away from administrative details that were better handled by deacons or by staff. These new elders had their ears to the ground. They were aware of hurting families both inside and outside the church, some with sensitive issues that needed attention. Their input changed the whole atmosphere of these monthly meetings.

What my ex-husband saw in the election of women elders was *power*—women trying to take control. Headship in his eyes constituted authority that women were forbidden to exercise. His mind was closed to the benefits of creational gender difference—*"male and female he created them"* (Genesis 1:27, emphasis added). He felt threatened by his own church, by women in general, and by a wife who celebrated these gender differences.

That a husband might feel threatened by an intelligent and articulate wife who speaks her mind could easily occur in an egalitarian marriage. But the man who insists the wife is under subjection is absolutely convinced that Scripture is on his side. And like my ex-husband, such men would typically have a significant gender advantage of physical size and strength. It's a muscular Christianity that holds the Bible in one hand and a clenched fist in the other.

Indeed, a clenched fist alongside a black-and-white Bible was figuratively my ex-husband's standard pose. The Bible—as he interpreted it—was the very Word of God, never to be challenged. For me, his belief in creation some six thousand years ago was not a problem as long as he did not make me subscribe to the same position. And what practical difference did it make in our everyday lives if we came to different conclusions on such matters? For him, the issue was my lack of submission to his views.

But the women's issue itself became the catalyst for most of his frequent explosions. My changing stance began slowly several years before women were elected as elders at our church. Even though I had taken a college course in biblical hermeneutics, it never dawned on me that I was accepting a traditional interpretation on women's roles without questioning its serious inconsistencies. But in the late 1970s, we moved to Michigan where we began teaching at the Grand

Rapids School of the Bible and Music. I was assigned to teach a course in women's ministries. The previous teacher had offered insights for pastors' wives and presented practical ideas on organizing women's meetings and mother-daughter banquets. My own failures along those lines pushed me toward historical and biblical topics. I hunkered down and read everything I could get my hands on.

Holy smokes. That was a dangerous turn. But I was, after all, teaching at a school that emphasized the Bible, and I had the full support of the president. What I discovered when I began digging into the most frequently referenced texts was that gender roles were not nearly as cut-and-dried as I had been led to believe. From Eve and Sarah to Priscilla and Phoebe, women had played critical roles, and I needed to give them a fresh look. Such was also the case with Paul's references to marriage and ministry. With my research under way, I was finding more and more serious scholars who were challenging long-held interpretations.

And I began to read the Bible differently myself, aided to at least a small degree by the two years of Greek I had taken in college. Greek scholars challenged me on certain critical passages such as 1 Timothy 2, which had long been the key text for restricting women's teaching and authority in the church. The fact that Paul in the same chapter takes a stand against women wearing jewelry and braided hair was mostly ignored by those who restricted women's roles in ministry. But that was not the issue on which I focused. I pointed my students to a much longer passage in chapter 5 of this same letter. There Paul goes on for fifteen verses, explaining exactly how older and younger widows should be regarded and supported or not supported by the community of believers.

Paul says nothing in the text that would indicate his concern for widows was merely a cultural issue that related to one particular church. Nor does he suggest that the matter related to women's teaching and having authority (however the verses were rendered) was written in stone for all time. Yet today we ignore this longer passage in chapter 5 and focus our attention on the few verses in chapter 2. In doing so, we are deciding which words of Paul's are important and which are not—an exercise in hermeneutics, always a human endeavor, and often seriously flawed.

One of the reasons a fresh hermeneutic is so critical is the inherent white male bias of past interpreters. That is not to say that men consciously interpret the Bible with a male bias. But historically, almost all biblical study was done by men, and their own traditional views of marriage and ministry naturally influenced how they interpreted the texts. David M. Scholer points to a typical example that relates to domestic violence. He cites an instance that clearly demonstrates the critical nature of this bias:

> On August 17, 1549, a Bible, fundamentally a new edition of the 1537 Matthew's Bible, was published in London by Jhon [sic] Daye, edited with notes by Edmund Becke. The most famous of all the notes in Becke's Bible is the one for the phrase, "Likewise, you men, dwell with them (your wives) according to knowledge" in 1 Peter 3:7. Becke annotated: "He dwelleth wyth his wyfe according to knowledge, that taketh her as a necessary helper, and not as a bonde servante, or a bonde slave. And yf she be not obedient and healpful unto hym, endeavoureth to beate the feare of God into her heade, that thereby she maye be compelled to learne her dutie, and to do it."[3]

Scholer goes on to say that "the idea that the Bible may justify and even encourage husbands to compel their wives to obey by force is, regrettably, deep within the tradition and life of the church and has shaped a painful reality for countless anonymous women throughout the last two millennia."[4]

Most of the biblical passages relating to women that are pounded into dust with hermeneutical hammers are found in the three opening chapters of the Bible and in Paul's letters near the end—pages 806–840 in my tattered desk Bible that ends on page 879. This leaves an awful lot of pages skipped over—pages that refer to marital relationships and ministry roles. Who decides what passages carry the most weight in speaking to gender issues today? Who decides which passages are to be taken literally? And who decides to ignore many of the Bible stories, relegating them to Vacation Bible School or an occasional topical sermon?

Let's look briefly at two biblical women—one obscure, the other quite well-known. The former, Junia, who is mentioned only once in Romans 16, has rated an endless stream of hermeneutical renderings. The latter, Sapphira, whose entire biblical life is boiled down to one episode in Acts 5, draws little attention from biblical scholars, though her story in some ways more closely ties into the subject matter of this volume and whose relationship with her husband should be observed as we contemplate headship and mutuality. Yet she is typically ignored.

Sapphira is married to Ananias, who owns property and decides to sell it. From the passage, it seems clear that she not only knows about the sale but also knows her husband intends to deceive Peter and the other apostles by claiming he is donating the entire amount of the sale for relief of the poor. As a result of their complicity, they are both struck dead—Ananias first and Sapphira three hours later. So here we have a married couple who, perhaps at the husband's suggestion, is concerned about a little nest egg for themselves. What if the heavy hand of Rome sends them all scattering? How will he support Sapphira and maybe children or grandchildren? But the expectation is that they, like others, would give everything to the apostles, who would then distribute the funds where most needed.

Ananias has the money in his pocket and is contemplating what to do. He has three choices: give it all to the apostles; give a portion, explaining that he's going to hold on to the rest; or, to avoid criticism, *tell* them he's giving it all while keeping the remainder. We are all human, and we understand his dishonesty. To us, the death penalty is overkill. But here is not the place to discuss that. Rather, the focus is on the wife and her agreement with her husband, who, in first-century Palestine, was legally the *ruler* of the wife. But in this case, the husband and wife are equally accountable before God. There is no "submission clause" that gets Sapphira off the hook. There was no recognized chain of command. That her husband was in authority over her wasn't worth a hill of beans when she was standing before Peter and the other apostles—and before the court of God's justice.

And who were these "apostles" that the text mentions? Are they the twelve apostles? That is the very issue that has launched Junia into the spotlight, particularly among recent biblical scholars. Paul would become the greatest of the apostles, and Junia, among others, is also referred to as an apostle. But who is this individual, a man or a woman?

Check her out on Amazon. Five books devoted to her pop up with a search of her name added to the word *Bible*. Eat your heart out, Sapphira! (No books feature *her*.) When you Google Junia's name, the 747,000 results are topped by Wikipedia's lengthy article. Quoted on both sides of the issue are dozens of biblical scholars, many well-known. As to gender, Wikipedia states, "The consensus among modern New Testament scholars is that Junia was a woman."[5] Indeed, that fight has been largely won. The big issue that remains is whether she was actually an apostle.

This entire debate centers around Romans 16:7: "Greet Andronicus and Junia, my fellow Jews who have been in prison with me. They are outstanding among the apostles, and they were in Christ before I was." It would seem from the plain reading of the text that Junia (and Andronicus, perhaps her husband) were apostles. But if we make her an apostle, the whole edifice of headship crumbles. So she must either be a man or be denied apostleship. Therein lies the dustup—a big debate over one otherwise very obscure woman.

His and her-meneutics. These debates are not about whether the Bible is actually the inerrant, infallible, inspired Word of God. Nor are they necessarily about *exegesis*, which relates more specifically to the translation of Greek or Hebrew words. Rather, these debates pivot on the interpretation of Scripture. Was Junia an apostle? Does it really

77

make any difference? Why should we care nearly two thousand years after the fact? But it does matter to women today if here in the biblical text we find a *woman apostle* working alongside Paul. And it matters to those who deny the legitimacy of women in ministry. The stakes are high. And the stories of Sapphira and Junia are relevant.

In the instance of Sapphira and her husband, Ananias, the matter was church discipline—the application of which we would surely today regard as excessive. On lying to Peter—or more specifically to the Holy Spirit—they both dropped dead. "Great fear seized the whole church and all who heard about these events" (Acts 5:11). Church discipline, by any standard is a controversial matter, though in this case the punishment was meted out by God, not man. Historically, the Inquisition stands as the most notorious club that meted out church discipline, and women were often in the crosshairs. But Protestants were also guilty. The Puritan church fathers in Salem, Massachusetts, hanged witches in the name of church discipline, as had been done in England and on the continent of Europe. And today church discipline is meted out by male elders, particularly in independent churches that require all members to sign a covenant.

In 2015, Karen Hinkley found herself on the receiving end of church discipline meted out by a council of male elders at the Village Church in Dallas. Led by Matt Chandler (often referred to as an evangelical superstar), the megachurch boasts several thousand members and many others who regularly attend. Those who join must sign a covenant that puts them under the authority of the elders, should discipline be deemed necessary.

Karen and her husband, Jordan Root, were on assignment as missionaries in Asia when Karen learned he was addicted to child porn. They both returned home, and he confessed his problem to the elders, who assumed they would be able to help repair this now-broken marriage. Karen, however, on learning that the addiction had been a major aspect of her husband's life long before they were even married, contacted an attorney and sought an annulment. If an

annulment means anything, this was an instance where it was appropriate. The couple had been married only a short time and had no
children. But the church elder board thought otherwise and placed
her under discipline after she had already asked that she be removed
from church membership.

After the story went viral, Matt Chandler apologized, but the episode illustrates so vividly the struggles that women confront among
those who exercise male headship in marriage and in the church.
Had she been treated fully as her husband's equal and had there been
women on that elder board, her awful position as a wife of a child porn
addict might well have been viewed in a different light.

Indeed, the accounts of Sapphira and Junia are telling. Sapphira
is not excused in the real estate transaction because her husband is
presumed head of the home and she is under his authority. Junia is
recognized by Paul to be among the apostles, one who has authority.
But when Karen faced discipline, she was presumed to be under subjection to her husband, and she faced an all-male elder board that had
not a single woman in authority who might identify with her plight.

How we interpret the Bible makes a difference. The stakes are
high. And the stakes were high in my marriage. In fact, my writing
and teaching on these issues added to an already complicated array of
marital problems.

On April 9, 1987, I wrote a journal entry about how my ex-
husband had several days earlier grabbed me late in the evening and
thrown me on the floor, shouting threats:

April 9, 1987

_I was thoroughly terrorized—as I never have been before. I truly
feared he might try to kill me ... [The next day] I called [his]
folks. I still was so filled with terror, and I guess I was grasping
at straws. They actually acted sympathetic, knowing [his] long
history of problems, but I should have realized they would try to
be defensive. They kept questioning me about little things such_

as church pledging, or particular Bible verses that we might have differences on that was causing [him] to go into such rages. They didn't want to see the whole picture, but rather to try to figure out little things that I could do to turn the situation around. [His] mother even suggested I go back to writing nursery school books.

Actually, while living in Crown Point, Indiana, I had written one such book, a coauthored volume titled *How to Set Up Your Own Neighborhood Preschool.* But Carlton was now twelve; years earlier, I had begun writing and publishing on subjects that were more closely related to my areas of expertise. Now I felt trapped. Here I was calling my in-laws, telling them I feared their son might kill me. His mother's only counsel: Set your academic writing aside and go back to writing nursery school books.

How did our marriage ever get to that point? When we met in the summer of 1968 on Word of Life Island, he learned immediately that I would be entering graduate school at Baylor University in the fall, and that I was, even then, intent on pursuing a PhD. His eyes were wide open. But so were mine. I learned from him that he had been expelled from Wheaton College and Miami Christian College and that he hoped to get into Shelton College in the future to finish his bachelor's degree. I learned that Carl McIntire, founder of Shelton, was one of my ex-husband's fundamentalist standard bearers, along with John R. Rice, both of whom were hard-line conservatives on religious and political issues. Despite our significant differences, we were both blinded by that fall in the Garden of Eden—falling in love in a paradise of perfection.

John R. Rice (who was awarded an honorary doctorate from Bob Jones University) was a radio preacher whose magazine *The Sword of the Lord* was for a time the loudest voice for American fundamentalism. He also wrote books, the most widely distributed being *Bobbed Hair, Bossy Wives, and Women Preachers.* In 1978 (the year we moved from Crown Point to Grand Rapids), he was still going strong, arriving at his office in Murfreesboro, Tennessee, at 6:30 every morning.

I recently came across some reflections by Stephen Lamb, the great-grandson of Rice: "I'm tired. Tired of the perennial discussions about the things women aren't allowed to do, or what a 'real man' or 'real woman' looks like," he writes. "Listening to claims from John Piper's *Desiring God Pastor's Conference* that God gave Christianity 'a masculine feel' . . . [makes me] realize that I no longer have any energy to debate those who hold to that position."[6]

In a 1979 sermon printed in his magazine, Rice railed against men for failing to assume their properly specified gender role:

> God bless good women. I am not blaming them. I am blaming you sissy-men, you panty-waists who have no conviction, no backbone, no character, no principle, no standards. You don't live for God. You don't have the convictions necessary to live for God. You don't stand. You don't have manhood enough. What we need these days in the matter of religion is godly men to take the place God assigned them in the church . . . We would not elect a woman president, nor follow a woman in business, but we leave church work to the women! No wonder the Bible said, "The children of this world are in their generation wiser than the children of light" (Luke 16:8).[7]

Sissy-men, panty-waists? Synonyms for Arnold Schwarzenegger's *girlie men?* I had never before heard anyone use the term *panty-waist.* On hearing John R. Rice deride men, it would be easy to believe that Mark Driscoll, onetime senior minister of Seattle's Mars Hill Church, was channeling him in some of his own tirades. Under an assumed name, Driscoll wrote this:

> We live in a completely pussified nation. We could get every man, real man as opposed to . . . crying Promise Keeping homo-erotic worship loving mama's boy sensitive emasculated neutered exact male replica evangellyfish, and have a conference in a phone booth. It all began with Adam . . . who kept his mouth shut and watched everything fall headlong down the slippery slide of hell/feminism when he shut his mouth and listened to

his wife who thought Satan was a good theologian when he should have led her and exercised his delegated authority as king of the planet.[8]

Were we to edit out the foul language spoken by Driscoll and gender slurs of Rice, are their concerns justified? Is masculinity today being threatened by egalitarian women? And has true femininity become as archaic as bloomers? My granddaughter Kayla, as a college freshman, has her sights on a career goal and is driven—so much so that she interviews for every freelance journalism job she can find. At the same time, she knows how to dress in feminine fashion and loves to tint her hair and pick out appropriate jewelry. She's feminine. And it has never entered her mind that somehow female is lesser than male. If guys are threatened by her, she considers it their problem, though her easy sense of humor is often like salve to a tender male ego.

One of the problems when one is dealing with masculinity and femininity is that these are cultural constructs, not biblical issues. In fact, femininity today is often closely associated with the kind of adornment Paul speaks against. And any attitude that emphasizes the he-man as "king of the planet" or a Christianity with a "masculine feel" is simply not biblical. Men who are secure in their manhood are not threatened by strong women. Indeed, a confident and capable woman can bring out the very best in a man. I point to John. He's never been threatened by his three strong, independent wives. He has no uneasy manhood to defend.

I celebrate gender difference, and I cannot even wrap my mind around wanting to be anything other than a woman. But the fact that women may have different ways of interpreting Scripture or different teaching styles or ministry priorities surely does not mean they are less capable than their male counterparts. It simply doesn't follow that gender difference makes women unfit for leadership and should therefore be under subjection to men in ministry and marriage.

Pope Francis spoke words of wisdom on the topic of gender difference when he was visiting the Philippines in January 2015. In this case, he recognized the problem of placing one gender above the other. In remarks made to an audience at a Catholic university, he lamented that only a small representation of females was present. His words that followed must have smelled like sweet perfume to the women— even sweeter perfume if he had hinted at moving toward opening the priesthood to women. (Mutuality in marriage is already an accepted tenet among Catholics):

> *Women have much to tell us in today's society.*
> *At times we men are too "machista" [the*
> *Spanish term for male chauvinists] . . .*
> *[We] don't allow room for women*
> *but women are capable*
> *of seeing things with a different angle from us,*
> *with a different eye.*
> *Women are able to pose questions*
> *that we men are not able to understand.*[9]

6

was john calvin a feminist?

Theologians and Women's Equality

Sincere Christians can disagree about
the details of Scripture and theology—
absolutely.

BILLY GRAHAM

It might have been a sixteenth-century Parisian love story—a
romance between Charles d'Espeville and Renée, a French princess. She was born in the autumn of 1510, he a year earlier. They
did not meet until the spring of 1536, however, when he visited her
home in Italy, staying on for a month. She was married with children;
he was single. But during that most extraordinary month, these two
strong-willed individuals began a long-term, long-distance relationship marked by admiration, affection, and, dare we say, abuse.[1]

The visitor with an assumed name was John Calvin; the hostess
was the princess of Ferrara. He had fled Paris, fearing for his life. She,
a budding secret Calvinist, gave him cover. Both were playing with

fire, risking their lives for the Protestant Reformation. Both had taken a stand against a powerful church that lacked conscience or qualms about burning or beheading a heretic.

After he left Ferrara, they carried on their relationship through secret correspondence. He stroked her with compliments, offering his "pure and true affection" for her. He pledged his undying loyalty, "myself a castaway if I neglected" you. But only so long as she remained loyal to him and his Reformed beliefs. She did—but not at the cost of losing her two young daughters.

Her husband, Duke of Ferrara, was the grandson of Pope Alexander VI, thus making Renée a choice religious plum for Calvin. When the Duke began to suspect his wife's Reformed leanings, he interrogated her. With her admission of guilt, he called in the palace guards. On September 17, 1544, she was locked (with her maid) in solitary confinement. Both little girls, Lucrezia and Eleonore, were taken to a convent. Renée was beside herself. What could she do to save herself and her little girls? Her mentor, Charles d'Espeville (a.k.a. John Calvin), had saved his own skin by surreptitiously fleeing Paris dressed as a farmer with a hoe over his shoulder. She had no such options. So she sent word to her husband that she would see a priest, say confession, and receive Communion. Soon she was free and reunited with her daughters.

How did Mr. d'Espeville, now in Switzerland, respond? With sympathy and relief, reminding her of how he himself had once fled the strong arm of the church? Did he quote Jesus: "Let the little children come to me, and do not hinder them"? Did he send her a box of Swiss chocolates? Hardly. He sharply reprimanded her: "I fear you have left the straight road to please the world . . . And indeed the devil has so entirely triumphed that we have been constrained to groan, and bow our heads in sorrow."[2]

Telling Renée that the devil had triumphed was heartless, implying she had made a Faustian bargain, selling her soul to the devil. Here is a mother desperate to do right by her young daughters, and he is castigating her, accusing her of leaving the straight road to please the world? What is this man thinking? Words do matter. They often come in the form of spiritual abuse.

John Calvin, love him or hate him. I confess that, like Renée, I have mixed emotions. It's not as though I can ignore him. My ex-husband proudly professed to be a "five-point Calvinist." My husband, John, who was born and raised in the Christian Reformed Church and taught for more than thirty years at Calvin College, is a *native* Calvinist (albeit, ambivalent about those five points). For more than a decade, I taught a course each year at the college and for six years was a professor at Calvin Theological Seminary. John Calvin, for better or for worse, is about as tangled up with me as he was with Renée.

For a number of reasons, Calvin is an important figure in this volume, and not only for the aforesaid connections. He has had an enormous influence on the American mind. And today he is the most respected—if not always revered—Reformation theologian among evangelicals. Most of the complementarians, dare I say without statistical support, profess to be Calvinists—or rather, *New* Calvinists. In fact, New Calvinism rated a 2009 top-ten spot in *Time* magazine's "10 Ideas Changing the World Right Now":

> In the 1700s, Puritan preacher Jonathan Edwards invested Calvinism with a rapturous near mysticism. Yet it was soon overtaken in the U.S. by movements like Methodism that were more impressed with human will . . .
>
> No more. Neo-Calvinist ministers and authors don't operate quite on a Rick Warren scale. But, notes Ted Olsen, a managing editor at *Christianity Today*, "everyone knows where the energy and the passion are in the Evangelical world"—with the pioneering new-Calvinist John Piper of Minneapolis, Seattle's pugnacious Mark Driscoll, and Albert Mohler, head of the Southern Seminary of the huge Southern Baptist Convention. The Calvinist-flavored ESV Study Bible sold out its first printing, and Reformed blogs like Between Two Worlds are among cyber-Christendom's hottest links.[3]

Most of these New Calvinists are Baptists or Independents with a Baptist flavor. Along with Calvin, Charles Haddon Spurgeon, a nineteenth-century Baptist megachurch preacher in London, is one of their heroes. But perhaps even more so is the New England Congregational preacher, philosopher, and theologian Jonathan Edwards. This is not the place for a review of Spurgeon or Edwards, but it is important to note that God's supremacy is a critical aspect of their theology. As such, they are heroes to John Piper and other New Calvinists. Regarding Edwards and Piper, Austin Fischer, minister and author of *Young, Restless, No Longer Reformed*, writes:

> I sat and watched the meticulous picture of God that Edwards and Piper painted. I loved so many of the strokes and colors. They finished painting, stepped back, and said, "What a masterpiece! The manifold excellencies of the glory of God, displayed in the doctrines of grace." I stepped back and said, "I really want to see that! . . . but I'm afraid I see a black hole instead."[4]

Here we see that the differences are not merely about how a wife should properly show deference to her husband. The central issue is a proper portrayal of a majestic and holy God. On the *Desiring God* website, the description of Piper's book *John Calvin and His Passion for the Majesty of God* places him and Calvin on precisely the same page: "John Piper fires readers' passion for the centrality and supremacy of God by unfolding Calvin's exemplary zeal for the glory of God."[5] This emphasis on the supremacy of God was Piper's primary focus when the two of us debated at Wheaton College. He argued that a husband's headship is based squarely on God's supremacy, though he did not claim then that Calvin had made the same case.

So was John Calvin a feminist? If not, was I trying to transform him into one, as my ex-husband charged me with doing? This issue became a major problem in our marriage. When I was in the editing process of my coauthored book *Daughters of the Church*, my ex-husband was employed as an editor at Zondervan Publishing House. My coauthor, Walt Liefeld, had written the biblical chapters and those pertaining to the church fathers. I had written the historical section, beginning with the medieval church.

Although my ex-husband was not the editor for this particular book, he obtained an unauthorized copy and concluded that I had not shown John Calvin to be sufficiently supportive of male headship. I explained that I had presented Calvin in traditional terms, while at the same time showing he was more nuanced than certain other theologians, and that I would not be changing the text. Later, he surreptitiously took the final edited copy and refused to return it until I had made changes according to his dictates. He also strongly objected to certain biblical interpretations and exegesis done by Walt.

Stealing a hard copy of a manuscript today would seem rather senseless since the entire manuscript is electronically stored and transmitted. Back in the mid-1980s, however, the theft was more serious.

I'll never forget flying into Chicago the morning after he had taken the manuscript. I was tense as my driver chatted while taking me to the seminary in Deerfield. After checking my mail and getting settled into my office, I found Walt and informed him of the problem. He immediately called Zondervan to assess the situation and make other arrangements. All this while I was preparing for my afternoon class. The flare-up the night before had left me drained. I feared having to return home the next day to more pent-up rage. I felt guilty and utterly ashamed for my part in slowing down the editorial process. I had tried so hard to become part of the seminary community and to cover up my traumatic home life. Now Walt knew, and other colleagues might find out too.

And how would I ever solve this crisis? Even if I had wanted to, I could never have convinced Walt to change his writing to pass my husband's inspection. The whole idea was absurd. How much easier life might have been had I stuck to subjects more suited to nursery schools. But had I even for a moment given such thoughts serious consideration, I would have realized that a violent man who terrorizes his wife is not mollified by a simple change in genre or perspective.

How would John Calvin have settled our situation back in sixteenth-century Geneva? Would he have told me to defy my husband? Perhaps, especially if I could use my influence to further the Reformed cause. After all, Calvin did encourage Renée to defy her husband in religious matters. Calvin needed a loyal supporter in Italy, and her loyalty to him trumped wifely submission to her Catholic husband.

Calvin played an entirely different tune, however, when a matter closer to home was brought to his attention:

> We have a special sympathy for poor women who are evilly and roughly treated by their husbands, because of the roughness and cruelty of the tyranny and captivity which is their lot. We do not find ourselves permitted by the Word of God, however, to advise a woman to leave her husband, except by force of necessity; and we do not understand this force to be operative when a husband behaves roughly and uses threats to his wife, nor even when he beats her, but when there is imminent peril to her life . . . We . . . exhort her to bear with patience the cross which God has seen fit to place upon her; and meanwhile not to deviate from the duty which she has before God to please her husband, but to be faithful whatever happens.[6]

In this instance, submission was required, even at the peril of a woman's own life. At the same time, Calvin's concept of "headship" in his personal life seemed to fall short of what is promoted today—the husband as *ruler* and *protector* of the wife.

With no *eHarmony* available, Calvin actually had difficulty finding a wife. He asked friends for help, and they obliged. But more than once, plans fell through. He made it clear in a letter to his friend William Farel that he was not one "of those insane lovers" who is "smitten at first sight with a fine figure." Rather, he was desirous of an "economical" woman who would be "interested about my health." When he did marry

Idelette de Bure, a young widow in his own church, he found neither health nor wealth. Her only "fortune" was her two children.[7]

After three difficult pregnancies (none of which resulted in a surviving infant) and a lengthy illness, she died only nine years after they were married. Calvin was heartbroken. He loved her deeply, and his onetime dream of finding a wife to tend his physical needs had been dashed. How different was Martin Luther's marriage to Katharina von Bora. She had escaped a Benedictine convent at age twenty-four. He was forty-one when they were married two years later. She was a strong and forceful wife who bore a brood of children.

But why waste words on biographical details when dealing with theological matters? Why should anyone care about Calvin's or Luther's or Renée's private life? Years ago, I read James McClendon's *Biography as Theology: How Life Stories Can Remake Today's Theology.* The book gave me a new perspective on the critical nature of biography when considering the underlying perspectives of a theologian. McClendon features biographies of four individuals, including Martin Luther King Jr., and shows how their lives informed their theology.

Key to McClendon's method is what he terms "a theology of character"—a "theology which incorporates the study of character—biography as theology."[8] McClendon is not the only scholar who has recognized the importance of biography in the study of theology. Other historians have drawn similar conclusions. For example, Philip Holtrop studied the lives and theological perspectives of Calvin, Beza, and Bullinger:

> They respected each other—but their temperaments seemed to shape their theologies in different ways. In a large part, theology is autobiography—and both are forged in the crucible of history. Genevan predestinationism was shaped also by personalities and historical contingencies—and not only by scholarship and biblical studies.[9]

We are far off the mark if we imagine that today's theological perspectives or those of decades or centuries past have little to do with the personality and character of the man or woman behind the pen or the podium. Indeed, when we listen to preachers, particularly those who have an ax to grind, we would not be off the mark to wonder how their theological perspectives are influenced by their personalities. Is the individual easily threatened and defensive? Such traits are revealing.

In his commentaries, John Calvin argues for the superior rank of the husband and the inferior rank of the wife as he believed was taught by Paul:

> He [Paul] establishes by *two* arguments the pre-eminence, which he had assigned to men above women. The *first* is, that as the woman derives her origin from the man, she is therefore inferior in rank. The *second* is, that as the woman was created for the sake of the man, she is therefore subject to him, as the work ultimately produced is to its cause. That the man is the beginning of the woman and the end for which she was made, is evident from the law.[10]

Though supported by Calvin in ignoring his "superior rank" argument and defying her husband's headship, Renée should not have been surprised that neither he nor those he sent to Italy to mentor her were open to the concept of gender equality. She had long resented having been passed over to succeed her father as the French monarch. "Had I had a beard I would have been the king of France," she fumed. "I have been defrauded by that confounded Salic Law."[11] Since her father had no sons to succeed him, Francis, Renée's third cousin, had ascended the throne. She was surely not unaware of other female monarchs, most notably Queen Isabella of Castile and co-monarch of Spain with her husband Ferdinand. And Isabella was succeeded by her daughter Joanna the Mad (who was apparently pushed over the brink into madness by her abusive husband). For the brilliant and strong-willed Renée, discrimination in the realm of politics had been a particularly bitter pill to swallow. But religious discrimination among the Reformers seemed like a wholly unnecessary slap in the face.

She strongly challenged François de Morel (sent to Italy to serve as her chaplain) about denying her a role in church decision making. He then wrote to Calvin: "Renée wants to attend the meetings of the synod . . . But if Paul thought that women should be silent in the church, how much more should they not participate in the making of decisions. How will the Papists and the Anabaptists scoff to see us run by women!"[12] Once again, her gender stood in the way. But she refused to be silent. Nor would she look the other way when she saw those in the Reformed camp committing atrocities against Catholics.

"Monsieur Calvin," she wrote, "I am distressed that you do not know how the half in this realm behave. They even exhort simple women to kill and strangle. This is not the rule of Christ. I say this out of the great affection which I hold for the Reformed religion."[13] Calvin refused to take responsibility, placing the blame on others.

It would be difficult to exaggerate the influence of John Calvin in religion (as well as culture). Puritans, Presbyterians, and Baptists of many stripes looked to his guidance long after he had passed from the scene. And his opponents were equally numerous. Among those who were forced to come to terms with Calvin since the sixteenth-century Reformation are three giants whose influence has nearly equaled his own: Abraham Kuyper and Karl Barth—who were considerably shaped by Calvin—and C. S. Lewis, who was not.

Abraham Kuyper was a leading Dutch politician, theologian, journalist, social reformer, and pastor whose influence has waned little in the century since his death in 1920. Calvin College, to name just one institution, would not be what it is today without the Kuyperian focus on integrating faith and learning—indeed, faith and every aspect of public life.

Karl Barth's name is almost synonymous with twentieth-century Protestant theology. Any serious theologian has had to come to terms with him, a man who some have suggested should be ranked alongside the church fathers. Although his so-called neoorthodoxy does not raise hackles among evangelicals as it did a half century ago, his works remain controversial.

C. S. Lewis, no doubt the most widely known of the three, profoundly shaped Christian thinking in the half century since his death. His influence on theological and biblical studies, however, is less clearly defined. What brings these three together in this volume is their strong stance against women's equality. They affirmed the traditionalist position of gender hierarchy in ministry and marriage. Their views have seeped into the evangelical consciousness. Indeed, it would be difficult to exaggerate their combined influence in this realm.

In many respects, however, these three twentieth-century giants pale alongside the mighty John Calvin, whose five hundreth birthday was celebrated in 2009. He stands alone in his religious influence over the modern world and over individuals such as myself. I had barely unpacked my bags when I arrived for my freshman year at St. Paul Bible College (now Crown College) when someone affronted me with the question, "Are you a Calvinist or an Arminian?" We argued endlessly, relishing every moment.

So back to my original question: Was John Calvin a feminist? Obviously he was no modern feminist, as I was accused of fashioning him. But he may have been more egalitarian than is typically believed. Of course, it depends on where one is quoting from Calvin. Here Mary Stewart Van Leeuwen's conclusions are worth considering: "If, as Calvin believed, men were mandated by God to be in authority over women in family, church and other spheres of society, this was simply for the sake of maintaining social order."[14] Van Leeuwen goes on to point out that Calvin was concerned about "decorum and edification"—as was Paul himself when, for example, Paul placed restrictions on women speaking in church (1 Corinthians 14:34). "The discerning reader," according to Calvin, would be able "to come to the decision that the things which Paul is dealing with here are indifferent," and thus would fall under the category of doing what does not give offense to the gospel. *Indifferent.* So is Calvin sitting on the fence?

How would Monsieur Calvin have reacted to recent changes in denominations that have historically most closely followed his teachings, namely, the Reformed Church in America and the Christian Reformed Church (where I have successively held memberships since 1985)? Would he have said that the decisions of both denominations to ordain women were *indifferent* and depended on decorum and edification and of not giving offense to the gospel? And how would he respond today to domestic violence as it is being dealt with by the Christian Reformed Church (CRC) today?

> In December 1989, the CRC's Synodical Committee on Abuse asked the Calvin College Social Research Center to survey adult members of the denomination to determine the prevalence of abuse in the CRC. About one in eight respondents reported having experienced physical abuse or neglect (12 percent) or sexual abuse (13 percent). Nearly one in five (19 percent) reported emotional abuse. In addition, 28 percent of respondents reported having experienced at least one of the three types. The survey yielded both qualitative and quantitative data for researchers and proved that church-goers are not immune to issues of abuse.[15]

In the quarter century since that time, the CRC in its annual synodical meetings has repeatedly revisited the subject, and more steps have been taken to ensure that abuse victims have channels of support. Although this denominational show of concern was not specifically focused on women who endure domestic violence, it goes without saying that an abused wife today in the CRC would not have to suffer a second time by hearing Calvin's altogether insensitive counsel: "We do not . . . advise a woman to leave her husband, except by force of necessity; and we do not understand this force to be operative when a husband behaves roughly and uses threats to his wife, nor even when he beats her."

It could be argued that Calvin was a man of his times, and one could imagine Martin Luther giving similar advice. In fact, while

Luther spoke against wife beating, he left the door open for such *discipline* if nothing else worked. But unlike Calvin, Luther was married to Katharina von Bora, a feisty former nun who talked back and never played the part of a subdued, subservient wife. When they first married, he judged her too proud. But what he took to be pride may have been her way of showing him she was not about to be stepped on. Their partnership was a marriage of mutuality, an interesting contrast to the marriage of John Calvin.

Martin and Katie set up housekeeping in the Black Cloister—a generous wedding gift from the Elector of Saxony. It was the onetime Wittenberg campus for the Augustinian friars. Katie was responsible for the administration of this large, rambling house (and hotel to a continual stream of traveling visitors), as well as the surrounding lands, where she raised and sold livestock, including cattle, pigs, goats, chickens, and geese (in addition to various household pets). She also maintained a brewery and often traveled to oversee still another farm at Zühlsdorf. Beyond those daily activities, she took charge of the on-site medical clinic, often full to capacity during epidemics.

That she reared six children and took in several orphans, in addition to lingering students, sums up her hectic life that easily parallels that of the Proverbs 31 woman. Is it any wonder that Martin spoke of her as "Dr. Katrina" and "My Lord Katie"? Her participation in lively discussions with students around the large table added an intellectual touch to her harried schedule. That he made derogatory remarks about her and women generally may say more about the steins of her beer he and his students consumed than his actual attitude.

"On one occasion," writes historian Ronald Fritze, "he put her on a search committee to hire a new pastor . . . To the grumblers Luther commented that his wife would show better judgment than he would. He also let Katherine handle much of his business with publishers. Frequently, Luther also took her advice on intellectual and political matters."[16]

To imagine Luther as a modern-day egalitarian would be inaccurate. He held, as did classical Greek philosophers, that women in theory were inferior to men. He drew his biblical support straight out of the story of Adam and Eve. He quoted Paul to make a case for denying women a voice behind the podium or pulpit. That position was standard biblical hermeneutics of the day, and there is no evidence that Katie resisted.

"No matter what Luther taught, no matter what Katharina accepted," write the authors of *Luther on Women*, "when the need arose Käthe took to the streets and marketplace, spoke out, doled out money to Martin, and ruled her household with as iron a fist as order demanded."[17]

Biography as theology—an interesting concept as it relates to Martin Luther and male headship. His and Katie's was an egalitarian marriage for all practical purposes, and it offers us a good example of a loving relationship of equals. Together they headed the first family of the Reformation, and their marriage, nearly five hundred years ago, stands as a model for today.

Luther's opening lines in a letter to her reveal as much as do his commentaries:

> *To my beloved wife, Katharina,*
> *Mrs. Dr. Luther, mistress of the pig market,*
> *lady of Zülsdorf,*
> *and whatsoever other titles may befit thy Grace.*[18]

the rule of thumb

Do Women Enjoy Equal Justice under the Law?

I long to hear that you have declared
an independency. And, by the way, in
the new code of laws . . . I desire you
would remember the ladies and be more
generous and favorable to them than your
ancestors. Do not put such unlimited
power into the hands of the husbands.
Remember, all men would be tyrants
if they could. If particular care and
attention is not paid to the ladies, we are
determined to foment a rebellion, and will
not hold ourselves bound by any laws in
which we have no voice or representation.

ABIGAIL ADAMS TO JOHN ADAMS, MARCH 31, 1776

Martin Luther King Jr. Day, 2015. Sybrina Fulton, the mother of the late Trayvon Martin, was the featured speaker for a day-long Dr. King commemoration at Grand Rapids Community College.

I heard about her address from an excited reporter, granddaughter Kayla, who is on the staff of the college newspaper. She edged her way forward after the event and had managed to get a few comments from Ms. Fulton.

For someone who has never lost a child, I cannot comprehend her sorrow. Only those who have entered that dark realm can understand. She stood her ground to give her message, as Kayla explained, but not without tears. Since that night when George Zimmerman killed her son and was exonerated by the courts, he has been back in court more than once on charges of domestic abuse, and one wonders why an abused woman doesn't simply stand her ground.

Indeed, a good question: Could an abused woman stand her ground and kill the abuser and walk out of court scot-free? A South Carolina case illustrates how callous some prosecutors are in cases of domestic violence:

> South Carolina is one of more than 20 states that has passed an expansive Stand Your Ground law authorizing individuals to use deadly force in self-defense . . .
>
> In the cases of women who claim they feared for their lives when confronted with violent intimate abusers, prosecutors say the Stand Your Ground law shouldn't apply . . .
>
> Most recently, [prosecutor Culver] Kidd raised this argument in vigorously pursuing a murder case against Whitlee Jones, whose screams for help as her boyfriend pulled her down the street by her hair prompted a neighbor to call the cops during a 2012 altercation. When the officer arrived that night, the argument had already ended and Jones had fled the scene. While she was out, Jones decided to leave her boyfriend, Eric Lee, and went back to the house to pack up her things . . . She packed a knife to protect herself, and as she exited the house, she says Lee attacked her and she stabbed Lee once in defense. He died, although Jones says she did not intend to kill him.
>
> On October 3, Circuit Judge J. C. Nicholson sided with Jones and granted her Stand Your Ground immunity . . .

Kidd . . . is appealing the case to argue that Jones and other defendants like her can't invoke the Stand Your Ground law so long as they are in their home.[1]

So here we have the February 26, 2012, killing of an unarmed black teenager shot by a heavyset twenty-nine-year-old man known for violence—no eyewitnesses—and he goes free based on his alleged fear for his own life. But in the November 1, 2012, killing of abuser Eric Lee, age twenty-nine, the prosecutor charged Whitlee Jones, age twenty-three, with murder—even though witnesses testified she was screaming for help when he was violently attacking her and even though she testified she was trying to protect herself.

I have studied neither case, but the very fact that Stand Your Ground applies in one case but not the other strikes me as seriously faulty justice. Historically, women have come out on the short end of the stick in the matter of justice—literally and figuratively, "rule of thumb" justice.

The rule of thumb: a husband may legally beat his wife with a stick no larger than the diameter of the base of his thumb. It was a law enacted by Romulus, the founder of Rome, hundreds of years before the Common Era, and it was made part of English common law that remained in force through the nineteenth century. True or false? The best historians now believe the entire story is mostly myth, a useful myth nonetheless. Most husbands have not needed a law to support their violence. If a case of abuse had gone to court, it was the husband's word against the wife's. As head of the home, he was typically counseled to be nice, she to be submissive.

The "rule of thumb" concept was cited by Harriet H. Robinson in her 1881 book *Massachusetts in the Woman Suffrage Movement*: "By the English common law, her husband was her lord and master. He had the custody of her person, and of her minor children. He could 'punish her with a stick no bigger than his thumb,' and she could not complain against him." More than a decade earlier, a court case, *State v. Rhodes*, found the husband innocent because he had "a right to whip his wife with a switch no larger than his thumb."[2] But historical studies have shown that the rule of thumb appears never to have been enacted as law, whether in ancient Rome, medieval England, or early America.

The rule of thumb, as outlandish as that may seem, implies discipline, as though a husband would carefully measure a stick or broom handle before he thoughtfully punished his wife. Such a scenario is not true to life and does not capture the scenes of domestic violence. More often, they are vicious outbursts involving beating with the fist or slamming the wife into the kitchen counter or onto the floor. I recorded in my journal some of these very incidents in the 1980s when we were living in Grand Rapids. At no time did my ex-husband's abuse remotely resemble measured discipline, even if we were to presume such "discipline" was the prerogative of a husband.

December 14, 1986

A week ago today we returned from NJ. It was a reasonably good trip going out, but the return trip was bad ... [He] and I were arguing about something when he hauled off and hit me on the side of the head. He was driving fast, and I feared an accident. I got out of my seat in a daze, moved to the back [of our VW Westfalia van], and in the process [he] began to violently swerve the van back and forth on the road. I was thrown around and hurt my hand and hip before I was able to catch myself and get seated. [He] demanded Carlton come up front with him. [He] and I had virtually no conversation after that—and it continues today—except for absolute necessities. My hip is black-and-blue and has ached through the night as I've tried to sleep.

December 21, 1986

Today has been a violent day ... Carlton saw it and picked up the phone to call the police. [His father] grabbed it out of his hands and tore it out of the wall and went back to hitting me. Carlton then grabbed a ball bat, threatening [him] if he continued to beat

me. [His father] then hit him and beat me some more and threw
me against the counter in the kitchen. He also knocked the door
off the hinges in the den. This has been the worst Carlton has
seen—he was extremely upset, threatening to do great harm to
[his father].

December 22, 1986

It's the morning after, and I am stiff and sore all over my body. I
had trouble sleeping because every time I moved, I felt the pain.
[He] did say he was sorry last night, and for the first time he
sounded willing to try to make the marriage work—allowing
me to have and express opinions that may be different from his.

Why didn't I report the abuse to law enforcement and contact an attorney at this time—or years earlier? More than anything else, I feared he would do what he had threatened to do—kill me. When I told him once after he had beaten me that if it ever happened again, I would call the police, his response was chilling: "That would be fatal." Carlton heard him and the next day accused him of threatening to kill me. He denied it.

But if I had reported the violence to law officers, wouldn't I have been protected? Some people do not realize there is little that law enforcement can do in such situations unless the woman is beaten so badly she is taken to the ER. Otherwise, it is typically her word against his, and he is warned not to beat her again. The most dangerous hours for any battered woman are those following a police visit to the home. And even if he is locked up for the night, he's back out as soon as he posts bond. Indeed, statistical studies have shown that more than 30 percent of "all women murdered in America are killed by their husbands, ex-husbands, or lovers."[3]

Such numbers are shocking in light of an 1871 Alabama law making it a crime for men to beat their wives. Other states soon followed. "Yet, for a century after courts repudiated the right of chastisement, the American legal system continued to treat wife beating differently from other cases of assault and battery," writes law professor Reva B. Siegel. "Men who assaulted their wives were often granted formal and informal immunities from prosecution, in order to protect the privacy of the family and to promote 'domestic harmony.'"[4]

No longer. Today the "domestic harmony" and "privacy" arguments carry far less weight—except among religious subcultures, including some conservative evangelicals. How did this change come about? "In the late 1970s," continues Siegel, "the feminist movement began to challenge the concept of family privacy that shielded wife abuse, and since then, it has secured many reforms designed to protect women from marital violence."[5] I was a beneficiary of that feminist campaign. By 1987, when I made my case before a judge, my story was all too believable. More women were graduating from law schools, some taking the cases of abused women pro bono and not being afraid to bring violent husbands into court. Others were stepping up to judgeships. Still other women were setting up crisis centers.

In 1994, as part of a federal Crime Victims Act, both houses of Congress passed the Violence Against Women Act. Though underfunded, it has provided training for law enforcement and court officials. Still, decades later, despite the progress made since the 1970s feminist initiatives, it is an understatement to conclude that *violence in the household persists.*

As much as modern feminism did to turn around public opinion and shine a spotlight on the crisis—this silent epidemic of domestic violence—many women in the nineteenth century risked far more to carry the message to an often-hostile public. In this realm, Elizabeth Packard stands tall. I cannot read her story without feeling chills up and down my spine. And to make matters worse, the story revolves around Calvinism. Why not some other belief system? Why don't Lutherans and Unitarians make the headlines?

It was no secret in the small town of Manteno, south of Chicago, that Elizabeth and Theophilus had some differences of opinion. He was the local Presbyterian minister, she his wife, forty-three years old and mother of their six children. But whatever gossip might have been spread in the late spring of 1860, it was overshadowed by the big news capturing everyone's attention. On May 18, Abraham Lincoln had been nominated in Chicago as the Republican candidate for president of the United States. Everyone in Illinois was chattering about sending their favorite son to Washington. Imagine that. People around town knew him personally or had heard him debate Stephen Douglas. Everyone had a story.

It was Monday morning, June 18, one month later. Mondays were marked as wash day. It was a long ordeal with a family of eight, scrubbing clothes soaked in a tub by hand on the washboard, rinsing them in another tub and hanging them out on the line, hopefully to blow in the breeze of a sunny day. But this would be no day of washing clothes for Elizabeth. The Reverend Theophilus Packard was taking her against her will to the insane asylum in Jacksonville, Illinois. Neighbors were stunned by the ordeal, and the children were crying out for their mother. But she had no recourse. "Married women," according to Illinois state law, "who in the judgment of the medical [Jacksonville] superintendent . . . are evidently insane . . . may be entered or detained in the hospital on the request of the husband . . . *without* the evidence of insanity."[6]

Indeed, under the law of the state of Illinois and under the law of God, Theophilus had no reason to doubt the rightness of his cause: "Illinois law had made him the arbiter of his wife's mental state, God's law made him the guardian of her soul. He was committing her to save her soul, to keep her from endangering the souls of their children, and to shield his creed from her criticism."[7] The theological issues went deep. The Packard differences were not spirited debates (of equals) on the merits of Calvinism versus Arminianism. Their disagreements were life-and-death matters that went to the very core of God's character. She would have none of her husband's harsh dogma. How could a loving God possibly send her little ones to eternal hell, even if they died in the very act of sinning, as in disobeying an order to stay away from thin ice on the pond? Nonsense.

Calvinism's God was supreme, as was Calvinism's husband. Male headship was the rule. Fairness was beside the point. Neither God nor husbands operated on a scale that took into account sympathy or sadness. So it was that the Packard children lost their mother, and Elizabeth lost her freedom. She was not without supporters, however. Theophilus was surely not the most popular man about town. In the days and months after Elizabeth's disappearance, neighbors knew exactly what was going on. In fact, Theophilus had grumbled about the circumstances himself: "I never saw children so attached to a mother," he lamented. "I cannot by any means wean them from her nor lead them to disregard her authority in the least thing . . . She seems by some means to hold them in obedience to her wishes just as much in her absence as in her presence."[8] His response was to forbid his children, ages eighteen months to eighteen years, to mention her name or try to contact her.

And what of Elizabeth, confined in an insane asylum? How did she survive the nightmare without actually going mad? Her reaction could be calculated in direct proportion to her sense of urgency to return to her children. Above all, she had to maintain her sanity. So she spent her time serving other women, who were in many cases actually insane, and she stroked the egos of administrators, sometimes in cordial conversations at their residence, dining at their invitation. When Dr. McFarland, the director, was questioned about her, he wrote that "for two years of the closest study . . . I could [not] discover any intellectual impairment at all, certainly nothing that deserves the name."[9]

Finally in June 1863, three years after her incarceration, Elizabeth was released, a result of appeals made by her oldest son and her sister, but not to freedom. Theophilus still had evil tricks up his sleeve. Back in her own home, he locked her in the nursery and boarded the windows in a misguided attempt to enforce God-ordained discipline.

Here she was, free to leave the institution only to be incarcerated in her own home unable to fulfill her role as a mother. Why, I ask myself, wasn't she set free by authorities to be a *despot* in her home, and why wasn't Theophilus arrested for unlawful imprisonment? I'm convinced Paul would have sided with her. His words in 1 Timothy 5:14 are revealing (though the situation he wrote about was entirely different from Elizabeth's): "I counsel younger widows to marry, to have children, to manage their homes and to give the enemy no opportunity for slander." On the surface, his directive seems like ordinary first-century advice. But his use of the Greek word *oikodespotēs* (the term for the wife's managing of the home) is striking.

I first learned about the radical nature of Paul's words through the writing of Katharine Bushnell (1855–1946). She was a medical doctor who served as a missionary in China and, perhaps more important for posterity, was a recognized biblical scholar. In reference to this passage, she writes:

> Men often talk of the father and husband as the "final authority" in the home. What says St. Paul on the point? The Greek word for "despot" (*despotēs*) furnishes us with our English word. Its meaning is precisely the same in Greek as it is in English. It means an absolute and arbitrary ruler, from whom there can be no appeal . . .
>
> *Oikos* is a very ordinary word in Greek, meaning "house." These two words, *oikos* and *despotēs*, unite to form the word *oikodespotēs*, which, as you can see, means "master of the house," and it is so rendered, Matthew 10:25; Luke 13:25; and 14:21.[10]

With the apostle's blessing, Elizabeth should have returned to her home and ruled as a benevolent despot. Instead, she was locked up. But she managed to slip a note out to a friend, who contacted a judge. No longer was the law on the side of Theophilus. The judge issued a writ of habeas corpus ("bring forth the body"). Now her case would go to trial before a jury.

The witnesses Theophilus asked to testify against his wife simply were not convincing. In Dr. Knott's opinion, she was "partially deranged on religious matters," though "on all other subjects she was perfectly rational." Dr. Brown testified that "she exhibited no special marks of insanity," at least in the realm of household affairs, but regarding her adamant denial of the Calvinist doctrine of total depravity, he declared with confidence that he "had not the slightest difficulty in concluding that she was hopelessly insane."[11] The jury deliberated for seven minutes. Elizabeth Packard was not insane.

Space does not permit sharing the rest of the story here, but her legacy has lived on. She was a strong woman, and in the years that followed, she became an activist for women's rights. Women in succeeding generations benefitted from appeals to elected political bodies throughout the country. Her legacy of activism was summed up in her obituary in the *Chicago Tribune*: "Through the influence of her books, added to her untiring efforts, thirty-four bills have been passed by various legislatures, each benefitting the insane in some way."[12]

In my book *Leadership Reconsidered*, I penned my own tribute to Elizabeth Packard:

> Elizabeth is to me a kindred spirit. I too was the wife of a staunch Calvinist minister in a small-town Illinois church. And much of the abuse she suffered I knew all too well. But thanks to Elizabeth and others like her, the laws had changed by the 1970s. Committing me to an asylum was not an option—except the asylum behind closed doors in our home. It was not until 1987 that I escaped with my thirteen-year-old son.[13]

When I escaped with Carlton, I sued for separate maintenance and full child custody. After I testified before the judge, my attorney called Carlton (who had been waiting in the hallway) to the stand. The first questions were easy, getting-acquainted inquiries. Soon, however, with little prodding, Carlton was describing violent scenes I'd all but forgotten. He expressed remorse as well as helplessness in his inability to defend me against his father. When the judge asked him how he felt about his father having joint custody, his answer jolted me. Almost as though he were prepared for the question, he said without hesitation that he would run away to Chicago—that a friend had told him about a place he could stay on the north side near Moody Bible Institute. *What is this all about?* I was thinking. But that statement, as much as anything else, clinched the judge's decision.

I did not sue for child support. I was well aware of my husband's violent episodes that were triggered by far less than something like court-ordered support. More than anything else in the weeks and months that followed, I feared he would kill me. And what did my ex-husband have to fear if he did kill me? Was there a serious deterrent in Grand Rapids in the late 1980s for wife killing?

In the months following my court action for separate main-tenance, I read about wives being killed. Then came the chilling headline of October 19, 1988. Judge Carol Irons had been fatally shot during lunch break in her court chambers by her police officer hus-band, Clarence Ratliff. Officer Ratliff was sentenced to two life terms for shooting at two other officers, putting shrapnel in one officer's leg. But for killing a sitting judge? The verdict was manslaughter. Two of the jurors who later defended their rationale said she had provoked him (by suing for divorce).

What did my ex-husband have to fear if he killed me? I was no sitting judge, and I had provoked him many times. Manslaughter? Maybe five to eight years, out early on good behavior? Wife killing in Grand Rapids, it seemed, was simply not taken seriously. Word quickly spread. The headline in the *Spokane Chronicle* on October 20, 1988, casually characterized this heinous crime: "Judge begs for help before hubbie shoots."[14] So how do we unravel this episode? Did wifey provoke hubbie before hubbie shot and killed wifey as she was begging for help? Shame on those jurors. And shame on the *Spokane Chronicle*.

But failure to bring justice can go both ways. We should not judge court cases, as is true with personal stories of abuse, simply with blind gender loyalty. Just because I oppose domestic violence against women, should I believe any woman's story without a serious investi-gation and sound hermeneutical principles? That is how it should be, and that is how I have viewed the court case against Officer Ratliff. I know the case well. He should have received a life sentence for killing his wife. But sometimes the situation is reversed. This is true in the case against Mary Winkler, though I view it at a greater distance and with less knowledge.

She was a battered wife who had no recourse but to stand her ground and kill her husband, so said her supporters. More than that, she was a preacher's wife. Bob Allen, managing editor of EthicsDaily .com, reported the following:

> Mary Winkler, a Tennessee preacher's wife who shot her husband dead in March 2006, received a sentence of 210 days in prison and three years probation after a jury convicted her of voluntary manslaughter based on her defense of abused spouse syndrome. Winkler was initially charged with first-degree murder after confessing to shooting her husband, Matthew Winkler, pulpit minister of Fourth Street Church of Christ in Selmer, Tennessee.[15]

When Pastor Winkler did not show up at a Wednesday evening service, church members went to the home, where they found his blood-soaked body. He had been shot in the back. The weapon—a 12-gauge shotgun. Mary was nowhere to be found, though later she was located in Alabama with her parents—her three children, ages one to eight, with her. She admitted that her husband was still alive when she grabbed the children and drove them out of state. Under questioning, Mary confessed that she killed him, adding, "I guess that's when my ugly came out." She also admitted that some of the marital difficulties they had were "her fault." In fact, she had become involved in a fraudulent Nigerian financial scheme without his knowledge. Her testimony was that of an abused wife: "He had really been on me lately criticizing me for things—the way I walk, I eat, everything. It was just building up to a point. I was tired of it. I guess I got to a point and snapped."[16]

In June, a grand jury indicted her for first-degree murder. A team of attorneys agreed to defend her pro bono. With their help, she posted bond and was released from jail in August.

The Wikipedia account states the following:

> On April 18, 2007, Mary Winkler took the stand in her
> own defense. She told a jury of ten women and two men that
> her husband often "berated" her and forced her to wear "slutty"
> costumes for sex. As proof, she displayed a pair of high-heeled
> shoes and a wig, at which those in attendance gasped.[17]

Men's rights groups were outraged by the non-guilty verdict.
But where were the women's groups? Why were they sitting on their
hands? Is there now open season on husbands who force their wives
to wear slutty costumes, high-heeled shoes, and a wig? Sure, family
members came to her defense, saying he had abused her. But where
was *his* voice in this trial?

A jury found Mary not guilty. I have no doubt this preacher's
wife got away with murder. And it's not just because I am able to
see Matthew Winkler as my own son, born in 1974, the same year
Carlton was born. Matthew's voice was stilled, his reputation sullied,
a congregation shocked, his wife set free. He was not only a preacher
but also the father of Patricia, Mary Alice, and Breanna. He was the
son of Dan and Diane Winkler, the brother of Daniel and Jacob.

Carol Irons was also much more than a professional—indeed, she
was a very successful attorney, who in 1982 became the first female
judge in Kent County, Michigan, where I have lived for nearly four
decades. This is where she tied the knot with Clarence Ratliff—a
garden wedding, a white dress. She looks happy in the photo posted
online. Referring to the garden, Pulitzer Prize–winning syndicated
columnist Ellen Goodman wrote the following:

> Here, too, the judge used to invite kids in for a talk, because
> she said, "I think schoolgirls ought to have professional women
> as role models."
> Now, dead at 40, she has become a different sort of female
> role model: a victim. She has become Anywoman who ever "pro-
> voked" a man into murder.

To this distant ear, the marriage between Judge Irons and Officer Ratliff sounds like a chapter out of "Smart Women, Foolish Choices." A second marriage for both of them, it didn't last long, and was followed by a rancorous separation . . .

An outraged friend of the judge, Noralee Carrier Potts, calls this "the-bitch-deserved-it defense." But, to be as frank as Carol Irons would have been, there is nothing unusual about this case. If the victim had not been a judge, the case might have passed unnoticed . . .

Last week in Grand Rapids, the men in Ratliff's motorcycle club, the Dillywackers, were saying to reporters, "If there were 10,000 Clarence Ratliffs, all the communists would dig holes and bury themselves."[18]

Goodman was correct in placing Carol Irons squarely among the smart women who make foolish choices. Carol had access to police records:

In 1975, Officer Ratliff broke into the home of his [first] ex-wife. Ratliff proceeded to pistol whip her, *"causing at least three lacerations"* in the back of her head. Ratliff was suspended from the department for five days for the assault.[19]

I did not know Carol Irons personally. I wish I had. She was a friend of my first attorney, who had done so much to calm my nerves and encourage Carlton, dropping my case only after she had been elected a judge and never billing me one dime for all her work. Through her, I felt a kinship with Carol, especially when I learned how she had gone to court at about the same time I was in court, both of us in an effort to escape violent marriages. I remember reading how she was spending time with friends trying to bring normalcy back into her life, taking piano lessons and joining a Bible study.

Many people in West Michigan called for renaming the district courthouse the Carol Irons Hall of Justice. Not surprisingly, it never happened. Ellen Goodman quoted one of Carol's friends and then added her own voice to that call:

"We have a right to expect zero tolerance toward domestic violence. There is no acceptable excuse. Not alcohol. Not adultery. There's no provocation for murder."
Write it on the walls of the Carol
S. Irons Hall of Justice.[20]

8

standing against cultural misogyny

Assessing Ethnic Differences

When you have caught the rhythm of Africa, you find out that it is the same in all her music.

KAREN BLIXEN, *OUT OF AFRICA*

Only ever so dimly did I catch the rhythm of Africa. And it was Kenya that captured my heart. Beginning in the 1980s, I had the good fortune of enrolling in cross-cultural courses in Kijabe. Actually, I was the teacher, though being a student was my goal. For each of four summers, I taught two courses at Moffat Bible College.

During that time, I learned far more than I taught my students. I credit that in part to my gender. In a short time, I was able to elicit students' opinions on various subjects—more so than seasoned professors. African students, at least back then, were often hesitant to offer an opinion that differed from that of the professor, particularly if the professor was a white male missionary. But challenging a woman was far less threatening. And if she was egging them on with controversial views, they couldn't resist the challenge. I might look back and regret that they did not accord me the same honor they accorded my male counterparts, but I don't—and I have no regrets.

A missionary who had previously taught at the school told me I should not expect class interaction. He advised me to be prepared to lecture for the entire session. I panicked. That simply is not my style. What was I going to do? And then came that first class. I can still picture the classroom. The eighteen students stared wide-eyed, not knowing how to act with this white American lady standing in front of them. It was a first for both of us. The course was church history, and I started slowly but soon was asking questions that related to their own experience and culture. *Had they experienced persecution or known people persecuted for their faith?* The lecture related to the second-century bishop Polycarp, burned at the stake for refusing to deny his faith. Soon we were dealing with church councils. What about African church councils? I wanted to know. I hadn't flown eight thousand miles just to listen to my own voice.

The class quickly livened up, especially as a Kikuyu or Kalenjin student might be arguing a point of Kenyan church history with a student from another tribe. And oh how often we all broke into laughter and into clucking, as they so endearingly did. I pushed and prodded. In fact, in this course and my other courses, we got into some very controversial topics. *What about the ordination of women?* So opposed were they to some of my ideas that they began ganging up on me. What fun! They were thinking aloud about certain issues for the first time, and I was having the time of my life.

That they argued strongly against women's ordination in class was not a sufficient rebuttal for certain students. They were determined to aim their guns, not just at me, but at anyone I may have influenced in the whole school. And, of course, word of my positions on such issues had quickly spread.

On my last evening before flying home to Grand Rapids, the students put on an all-school program, singing all my favorite Swahili gospel songs and ending with a skit. One of my male students dressed in drag as a woman preacher—and not just that, but as a very pregnant woman preacher. Sure, she could preach and even win converts, as he adeptly demonstrated, but could she perform a baptism? Here was the crux of the matter. When she waddles down into the imaginary river to lower the hulking male convert into the water for baptism, she falls in and struggles with all her might to regain her footing, as well as her composure. The baptism is thwarted. To the howls of laughter, the case had been closed. A woman cannot be ordained to the ministry.

If I had the space, I would tell dozens of stories about my wonderful days in Kenya when I learned firsthand how different one culture is from another—and how different even one tribe is from another. I learned quickly how proper behavior in one culture can be seen as entirely inappropriate in another.

I was shocked, however, by how easily some of my male students defended wife beating—though, they insisted, only if the wives deserved it. But before I pronounce a blanket condemnation on Kenyan culture for wife beating (and the defense of it), it is important to acknowledge that they had their own means of dealing with such abuse. My students were quick to counter my strong opposition to any form of violence. They insisted that such *discipline* was not hurtful and that when the husband stepped over the line, the wife had a powerful recourse. She would tell her family, and her father and her brothers would go to her husband's family and the matter would be settled. The husband would not dare to hit her again.

We might roll our eyes at such justice, but when it worked effectively, it may have been more efficient and effective than the American justice system was back in the 1980s when I was being beaten. Such family justice is cultural. It could rarely work in a typical Western culture where a young couple lives behind closed doors at a great distance from either side of the family. And Americans are secretive. A father would be the last person a young wife would likely tell about the abuse she was suffering.

One of the most memorable lessons on American attitudes toward privacy came years later when John and I were teaching a course at Saints Bible Institute in the Italian village of San Lorenzo. Sam Spatola, the founder and president, is warm and friendly, always eager to answer questions and show visitors around town. As we were out strolling the streets together one evening, he pointed out new construction and how difficult it was for the wealthy homeowner to put a large addition on his house without bumping into the houses on all sides of him, packed as they all were in less than an acre of land. Then he made an unrelated comment about this same man and pointed to a tract of land he owned a block away, separate from the village proper. I asked why the man didn't simply build a new house in that very lovely, tree-lined setting. Sam, genuinely confused by my question, said what he thought should have been obvious: The man wanted to live in the village right next to everyone else.

Not in America. We don't want to live right next to everyone else. If we're rich, we purchase a large tract of land and build our big house at the end of a long paved driveway, trees shrouding us from potentially nosey neighbors.

Our worldviews, typically formed in a particular culture or subculture, function like a pair of glasses, and we often assume our way of seeing is the right way. But my cultural individualism is not the norm for others around the world. Nor is it true of biblical culture from beginning to end. Individualism rarely comes to the fore. Indeed, we can learn a lot about culture and cultural norms from Scripture.

The apostle Paul, more than any other biblical figure, is conscious of cultural considerations. He is, first and foremost, a missionary, and he travels far beyond his hometown of Tarsus, itself hardly a backwater, monocultural city. In fact, Tarsus boasted a large port and was one of the busiest trading centers on the Mediterranean Sea. If there was a missionary or missiologist today who surpassed Paul in the theory and practice of cross-cultural contextualization, I'm sure she would be too embarrassed to claim as much. He stands alone. When he was ministering to people who believed and behaved differently, he *mirrored* them, as he wrote in his first letter to the Corinthian church:

> To the Jews I became like a Jew, to win the Jews. To those under the law I became like one under the law . . . so as to win those under the law. To those not having the law I became like one not having the law . . . To the weak I became weak, to win the weak. I have become all things to all people so that by all possible means I might save some.

> 1 CORINTHIANS 9:20–22

Paul put his principles into practice when he was in Athens. Here he is in the midst of scoffers, particularly Epicurean and Stoic philosophers. He might have stood on a soapbox and simply preached Jesus. Instead, here in Athens, he became an Athenian and lectured where these very philosophers presented their own views. The episode is captured in Acts 17:22–23:

> Paul then stood up in the meeting of the Areopagus and said: "People of Athens! I see that in every way you are very religious. For as I walked around and looked carefully at your objects of worship, I even found an altar with this inscription: TO AN UNKNOWN GOD. So you are ignorant of the very thing you worship—and this is what I am going to proclaim to you.

Paul preached to the onlookers and ended his sermon by quoting familiar pagan poetry: "'For in him we live and move and have our being.' As some of your own poets have said, 'We are his offspring'" (Acts 17:28). He was very conscious of not offending people and thus being a stumbling block to the gospel. In fact, many of his proscriptions regarding gender fall into this very category. Would Paul, if he were headquartered in Grand Rapids, be concerned about hair length today? Would he be upset that a prominent preacher wears his hair long? Would he even take notice that the wife of a leading complementarian wears her hair short and stylish? Hardly. Yet he wrote in his first letter to the Corinthians about this very matter, no doubt due to cultural considerations: "Does not the very nature of things teach you that if a man has long hair, it is a disgrace to him, but that if a woman has long hair, it is her glory? For long hair is given to her as a covering" (1 Corinthians 11:14–15).

We easily pick and choose which verses are written in stone to be rigidly followed forever and which are culturally conditioned. Chapter 2 of Paul's first letter to Timothy is a case in point and much debated. Here Paul mentions many things that appear to be as culturally conditioned as hair length: Men are to "lift up holy hands" when they pray. Women are to "dress modestly," strictly avoiding "elaborate hairstyles or gold or pearls or expensive clothes." Women are to "learn in quietness and full submission" and are not permitted to "assume authority over a man." Paul ends the passage by saying that "women will be saved through childbearing."

The first thing we note is that Paul seems far more concerned about the *propriety* of women in this first-century faith community than he is about the propriety of men. Right there is a dead giveaway. First-century Palestine, where the Christian faith was born, had far more restrictive rules for women's public and private behavior than for men's. Paul goes along with those cultural mores so as to avoid causing an offense to the gospel, while at the same time endorsing women in ministry. Regarding hair, jewelry, and clothes, his concern may have been partly related to the sins of every era: pride and materialism. That women learn in quietness and not exercise authority over men was part and parcel of first-century propriety.

That women will be saved through childbearing is a statement that almost every Bible commentator seeks to explain, though never in my mind to any degree of satisfaction. When I come to that verse, I leave Paul to his own rumination, and skip on by.

The most controversial cultural issue that Paul confronted head-on was circumcision. For Jews, the matter was nonnegotiable. It was the bedrock sign—more than that, a covenant—of being a chosen people, a required rite since God spoke the very word to Abraham.

There was no room for compromise. Paul, himself circumcised, was a missionary to the Gentiles, and his insistence that circumcision was not necessary to become part of the *new covenant* squared with his contextualizing methods.

"If Paul had simply affirmed cultural distinctives and viewed them as points of contact for inculturating the gospel, his approach to culture would have been quite straightforward," writes Dean Flemming. But "Paul believes that God has done something radically new in Christ that signals an end to the old order of things . . . He calls the Galatians to perceive the world in a radically different way from the default setting of their culture."[1] Here, Flemming references Paul in Galatians 3:28:

> There is neither Jew nor Gentile,
>> neither slave nor free,
>> nor is there male and female,
>> for you are all one in Christ Jesus.

These twenty-four words (in the NIV) form what Paul Jewett termed the "Magna Carta of Humanity." Theologian and biblical scholar Klyne Snodgrass captured the significance even more forcefully, calling this "the most socially explosive statement in the New Testament."[2]

Paul has a two-pronged focus regarding cultural considerations. While emphasizing contextualization in mission outreach, he at the same time boldly proclaims that Christians must perceive the world *in a radically different way from the default setting of their culture.* A default setting throughout history and infiltrating every culture has been the demeaning of women. Demeaning leads to degrading, degrading to revulsion, and revulsion to hatred (or misogyny). I became aware of such cultural hatred after I first arrived at the large mission outpost of Kijabe, Kenya, in 1985. Fifty-five years earlier, a terrible atrocity had been committed right there in that mission setting. Dana Robert succinctly sums up the violent episode:

In early 1930, sixty-four-year-old single missionary Hulda Stumpf was forcibly "circumcised" and murdered in her home at the central mission station of Kijabe, Kenya. A trained stenographer, she had served the mission for twenty-four years. She had worked with girls and taken care of much of the business correspondence at the Kijabe Station. Irascible, hard of hearing, and living alone, she had taken one of the firmest stands against female circumcision in the Kijabe Girls' school.[3]

The term now used for this widely practiced cultural rite is "female genital mutilation" (FGM), and Hulda was outraged by the practice. A business school graduate, she was more than a nice lady who could take dictation and write shorthand. In fact, before joining the Africa Inland Mission, she taught at the Indiana Business College. Although she was marginalized by her single-woman status, she was determined to speak her mind on the matter of mutilating girls—girls in the very school where she taught. But her stance was controversial. Girls, without this horrendous rite, were regarded as outcasts and unmarriageable. But Hulda was fully aware of the pain and permanent injury that the "ceremony" entailed, described in detail in a memorandum distributed by the Church of Scotland Mission only one year before she was murdered:

> Female circumcision, as it exists among the Kikuyu, is an operation which varies in severity, some sections of the tribe practicing a more drastic form than others. It involves the removal of not only the clitoris, but also the labia minora and half the labia majora, together with the surrounding tissue, resulting in the permanent mutilation affecting the woman's natural functions of maturation, menstruation, and parturition, with disastrous results not only to the birth rate, but also to the physique and vitality of the tribe.[4]

Hulda Stumpf was certainly not the first missionary to take a stand against this practice. In fact, in 1914, the Africa Inland Mission clearly stated its strong opposition. But as a single woman, she was seen by certain Kikuyu tribal leaders as a threat to their way of life. So it was, then, that on January 3, 1930, she was strangled in her own tiny house. The inquest into her death also concluded: "Medical evidence shows that Miss Stumpf was circumcised in brutal manner and died under the operation."[5]

I learned while I was teaching in Kenya how prevalent the practice still was. Although some have argued that it is a legitimate African rite, it is important to point out that a critical motivation for this *man-made* rite is to prevent girls from having sex before marriage. Being "sewed up," however, does not prevent rape. And for the married woman, the mutilation removes pleasure from sexual intercourse. It is a demeaning and degrading and often hateful act—though carried out by a tribal woman practitioner.

Years ago when I was teaching a women's ministries course at Trinity, I was called into the academic dean's office. One of my students had complained to him that she had become ill—had gotten sick to her stomach and almost fainted—as a result of an ABC *20/20* episode on FGM that I had shown in class. The dean wanted to hear what I had to say. I was *guilty as charged*. My point was not to have students leave class but to wake them up to atrocities against women in the name of cultural norms.

Although the documentary focused on Africa, it also showed how FGM had become an issue in America. Since then, the crisis has grown. A federal law in 1996, followed up by laws in many states, made the practice illegal. But according to reporter Nina Strochlic, "New numbers show that these measures have done little to stanch the skyrocketing rate at which girls are subjected to this cruel form of circumcision on our shores." In 1997, the first year that statistics were available, some "168,000 girls and women were at risk or had undergone FGM." The latest figures, as reported on February 4, 2015, show there were "around 507,000 girls living in the U.S. who are either at risk of being cut or who have already been cut. That's more than triple the figure from the very first nationwide count."[6]

It is easy to point a finger at African culture, though in the case of FGM, the finger-pointing is warranted wherever such a violent act against girls and women is committed. But American culture has also spawned its own unique forms of degrading women, and it is not necessary to search nineteenth-century archives to find them. One such degradation relates to popular music, particularly rap and hip-hop.

But before I launch into a condemnation of the often-misogynist lyrics glorifying violence against women, I call to my readers' attention the backlash that Tipper Gore (wife of vice president Al Gore) confronted when she spoke out on the issue. She was accused of calling for censorship, even though her 1990 *Washington Post* editorial was very modest in its plea for the music industry to put labels on albums that were not appropriate for children. More than that, she was accused of being an old white lady (only forty-two at the time) who was interfering in a matter she knew nothing about.

In light of that, my words obviously mean nothing among those who are involved in this "lyrical misogyny." But others do have a platform, including President Barack Obama, who prerecorded a message for the 2015 Grammy Awards. Clover Hope later recounted his public service announcement: "President Barack Obama interrupted the predictably boring Grammy Awards tonight to spread an important message on rape and domestic violence. Amidst the standard awards show proceedings, it made for a jarringly real moment." She then quoted from his speech:

> Tonight, we celebrate artists whose music message helps shape our culture and together, we can change our culture for the better by ending violence against women and girls. Right now, nearly one in five women in America has been a victim of rape or attempted rape. And more than one in four women has experienced some form of domestic violence. It's not okay. And it has to stop. Artists have a unique power to change minds and attitudes and get us thinking and talking about what matters. And all of us, in our own lives, have the power to set an example.[7]

Apart from reading some of these lyrics filled with obscene and vicious threats against women, I know very little about this subject, and my voice counts for even less. But the president's message, followed that night by the testimony of an abuse survivor and the singing of Katy Perry, does count for a lot. Katy's song "By the Grace of God" encourages abused women to "put one foot in front of the other" to look into "the mirror" and not "let love take me out that way." A black president and a superstar singer have voices that are far more difficult to mock than Tipper Gore's and my own. We can only hope that all forms of media will take the message to heart and, step-by-step, help to turn the industry around.

Unlike female genital mutilation, misogynistic lyrics are not in themselves physical violence against women. One relates to a long-standing practice—or rite—carried out in patriarchal societies, the other a contemporary fad or "rite of passage" protected by the Bill of Rights. While it is critical that we recognize cultural differences, we must at the same time condemn misogyny wherever it is found, whether in cruel cultural traditions or in contemporary trends in pop culture.

Indeed, one does not have to go to Africa or become embedded in the rap music industry to encounter the culture of misogyny. From the ancient Greek and Asian societies to medieval Catholicism and Enlightenment Europe, we find strands of misogyny in every facet of life. And that culture of misogyny is alive and well today. I felt its ever-present oppression in my previous marriage. In fact, one of my journal entries speaks directly to this issue.

September 8, 1986

This morning I turned on Donahue, and the subject was misogyny. A book by Dr. Susan Forward, Men Who Hate Women, was being discussed, and [my husband] seemed to fit all the characteristics—charming and personable in public, but demanding complete control in the home. I almost think he is an extreme case.

I sometimes asked my ex-husband, "Why do you hate me so much?" He would say he didn't hate me but would add that my lack of submission made him respond in hateful ways. Justification enough. And it was not just me. He appeared to hate women in general. He would make gender slurs about groups of women, as well as about certain individuals. If he happened to disagree with a woman on any particular matter, he would hiss that she was a *feminist*. They might have been very traditional in their views on gender, but they were strong women who happened to rub him the wrong way.

Misogyny. Men who hate women. This *culture of hatred* is found among religious and nonreligious alike. But what is truly astounding is that it is not infrequently seen among those who demand that women be subject to men, basing that obligation on Ephesians 5. What stands out in the passage is that husbands are directed to *love their wives, just as Christ loved the church*. We must be cautious about throwing the term around too casually, but at the same time we shouldn't be afraid of the word *misogynist*. How do we know if a man truly is one? "I love the pretty girls," he says. So we assume he can't be a misogynist. But "loving the pretty girls" might be a telltale sign of misogyny. *Control* is a key. Whether it's African mutilation rites or rap music or marital abuse, the demand to domineer is always present. Yet hatred of women is not easily detectable. Indeed, there is a fine line between male domination and misogyny. And the term *misogynist* that refers to one individual should not be used apart from the phrase *culture of misogyny*—a culture that rears its ugly head even in Scripture.

So now for the critical question: *Was the apostle Paul a misogynist?* This is the title of a 2015 *Christian Post* column by Richard Land, a Southern Baptist and the president of Southern Evangelical Seminary. He begins with these words: "In the modern world many people rather casually assume, or assert, that the Apostle Paul was a misogynist based upon his teachings concerning the differing roles of men and women in the church and in marriage in the early church."[8] Actually, Land's charge is somewhat overdrawn. But the issue is worthy of consideration.

Critics of Paul, including Pearl S. Buck, presumed he hated women. In reflecting on her mother and on her domineering father, Buck wrote, "Since those days when I saw all her nature dimmed I have hated Saint Paul with all my heart and so must all true women hate him, I think, because of what he has done in the past to women . . . proud free-born women, yet damned by their very womanhood."[9]

I find it almost incomprehensible how anyone who has ever actually read the writings of Paul, as Pearl Buck did, could argue that he damned women for their very womanhood—that he was a misogynist. There is nothing in his writings that suggests he hated or wanted to control women. If Paul were around today, I am convinced he would be the last person to write a book or lecture at a podium calling for the restriction of women in ministry or marriage.

And Pearl Buck, of all people—misinterpreting his position on matters that are culturally conditioned. She was a missionary herself and a remarkably keen observer of China. Didn't she recognize how Paul walked a tightrope between cultures? Didn't she realize that what appeared to be restrictions on women were in many cases opening doors and actually paving the way for them to work side by side with him in ministry? Indeed, Pearl Buck wrote one of the most perceptive books I know on cultural understandings of China. Years ago while traveling alone, I listened to the unabridged version of her Pulitzer Prize–winning *The Good Earth* and came away marveling at her insights.

But I stand against her in her assessment of Paul. He repeatedly praised his female coworkers for their faithful service. He surely did not hate women.

Men Who Hate Women is a title designed to grab readers' attention (and it does not assume there are not women who hate men). Rarely, however, have I encountered a man I would label as a misogynist, though I know such an attitude can be disguised. The greater concern ought to be the misogyny that seeps into the very fabric of culture. Those most susceptible are those, like my ex-husband, who place severe restrictions on women. Indeed, the demand for subjection opens the door to hatred—hatred aimed at the one who stands against that demand. Alongside such hatred of women is an attitude that sees women as lesser. It is an attitude that prefers the company of other men.

My husband, John, is just the opposite. He does not need to stand in a stadium and shout, "I love women!" (as Ann Romney did at the 2012 Republican convention). It's simply part of his makeup, whether he is watching the evening news or in the midst of a group of women at church. It's not something that in any way draws attention. Rather, it is wrapped up in his character. And wasn't Jesus that way? Dorothy Sayers's oft-quoted description of Jesus says it all:

> Perhaps it is no wonder that women were first at the Cradle and last at the Cross. They had never known a man like this Man—there never has been such another. A prophet and teacher who never nagged at them, never flattered or coaxed or patronized; who never made arch jokes about them, never treated them either as "The women, God help us!" or "The ladies, God bless them!"; who rebuked without querulousness and praised without condescension; who took their questions and arguments seriously; who never mapped out their sphere for them, never urged them to be feminine or jeered at them for being female; who had no axe to grind and no uneasy male dignity to defend; who took them as he found them and was completely unself-conscious. There is no act, no sermon, no parable in the whole Gospel that borrows its pungency from female perversity; nobody could possibly guess from the words and deeds of Jesus that there was anything "funny" about woman's nature.[10]

9

fifty shades of rape

Is There Ever Legitimate Rape in Marriage?

> I say nothing, not one word, from
> beginning to end, and neither does he.
> If it were lawful for a woman to hate her
> husband, I would hate him as a rapist.
>
> **PHILIPPA GREGORY, *THE RED QUEEN***

Legitimate rape. Not in the eyes of Saint Augustine. When he discoursed on the subject, he put the blame squarely on the man. He was not referring to an actual rape, but rather to the Roman legend of "the Rape of Lucretia." What troubled Augustine was that after she is raped, Lucretia performs the only honorable act available to her. She kills herself. In *The City of God*, Augustine strongly objected to her suicide, for "when a woman is violated while her soul admits no consent to the iniquity, but remains inviolably chaste, the sin is not hers, but his who violates her."[1]

William Shakespeare brought a new perspective to this ancient Roman legend in his lengthy poem "The Rape of Lucrece." In his retelling, Lucrece regains her voice after the awful rape, refusing to take any responsibility upon herself.

"This first revelation of her own authorial power propels Lucrece to spring into physical action to take charge of her destiny," writes Laura Stampler in her honors thesis at Stanford University.[2] Lucrece struggles, however, in how best to claim her innocence, whether postponing her suicide or not killing herself at all and keeping the crime a secret. "Through lengthy inner struggle, Lucrece determines that she will not suffer her fate alone and allow the crime that has been committed against her to go unpunished."[3] In the end, she does the "honorable" thing and commits suicide, but not before she has told her husband and has the assurance that he will take revenge. But the moral of this narrative poem is that Lucrece has found a voice that can never be stilled. She tells her story publicly, while acknowledging that her chosen path will still lead to her suicide. Lucrece says to her servant:

> . . . if it should be told,
> The repetition cannot make it less;
> For more it is than I can well express . . .
> Go get me hither paper, ink, and pen.[4]

Go get me hither paper, ink, and pen. This should be the motto of all those who suffer domestic violence and rape. Like Lucrece, we are tempted to vacillate, doubting ourselves. But like her, we must claim our own voice. Unlike her decision, as Augustine so strongly declares, choosing to commit suicide is the wrong course.

The term *legitimate rape* entered the American lexicon in August 2012. That was when Missouri Republican congressman Todd Akin told a reporter that a pregnancy resulting from rape is "really rare." He added that "if it's a legitimate rape, the female body has ways to try to shut that whole thing down."[5]

Where might Akin have come up with this wacky theory that the female body can "shut that whole thing down"? His conclusion in the eyes of almost everyone was utterly laughable. But maybe he had a solid source backing him up. Had he been reading the ancient legend of "the Rape of Lucretia"? If he had, he might have learned that it was presumed in ancient Rome that if the raped woman became pregnant, she was actually an agreeable—if not eager—participant in the sexual encounter. So would hers then have been an *illegitimate rape*? By Akin's definition, yes.

No scripture of any religion features more stories of rape than does the Bible. Some of these accounts are chilling and difficult to comprehend. We ask ourselves, *How could God's people commit such awful crimes and go unpunished when far lesser crimes are severely dealt with?* Others have written about these "texts of terror," which I will not review here. But even the laws regarding rape are downright confusing, particularly those that appear in Deuteronomy 22:23–29:

> If a man happens to meet in a town a virgin pledged to be married and he sleeps with her, you shall take both of them to the gate of that town and stone them to death—the young woman because she was in a town and did not scream for help, and the man because he violated another man's wife. You must purge the evil from among you.
>
> But if out in the country a man happens to meet a young woman pledged to be married and rapes her, only the man who has done this shall die. Do nothing to the woman; she has committed no sin deserving death. This case is like that of someone who attacks and murders a neighbor, for the man found the young woman out in the country, and though the betrothed woman screamed, there was no one to rescue her.
>
> If a man happens to meet a virgin who is not pledged to be married and rapes her and they are discovered, he shall pay her father fifty shekels of silver. He must marry the young woman, for he has violated her. He can never divorce her as long as he lives.

We simply want to shut these laws down. They are too cut-and-dried and make seemingly simplistic assumptions that there are no other extenuating circumstances. What if the woman in the first instance had tried to scream for help but was prevented from doing so? In the second instance, the woman gets a break, and we are relieved that "she has committed no sin deserving of death." And, in fact, her report of the rape is deemed hard evidence. In the third scenario, the young woman is forced to marry the man who raped her, apparently even if she had screamed for help. As frequently as it references rape, the Bible does not present the woman's point of view. The description comes through the voices of men.

Describing rape in its ugliest form pummels the reader with unsightly blood and the raw, piercing throb of pain that no wail or cry can capture. The sounds that do deafen the readers' ears are those awful, indescribably degrading rapist slurs and obscenities that puncture the soiled, stinking air.

One poet who speaks profoundly on rape is Samantha Coerbell in her 1999 poem titled "The Romanticization." The pretense of romance is indeed sometimes how rape begins:

> *And when he said to me*
> *"Honey, you will be my only one" . . .*
> *I believed*
> *He would take me in his arms . . .*

The more than three thousand words that follow describe rape that is too graphic to quote. The reader can look up the poem online or try to imagine the utter depth of awfulness. In the end, when the hateful physical violence is over, the victim again *believed*.

> *the only ringing*
> *was in my ears*
> *When he said*
> *"Whore, I should kill you"*
> *I believed.*[6]

My own account of rape, if, in fact, it was *legitimate* rape, was not a violent, physical episode saturated with blood and piercing pain or even punctuated with obscenities. But it was a scene of soiled, stinking air—an ugly episode of hateful, "God-ordained" domination and supremacy, wholly devoid of the sweet fragrance of delightful sexual intimacy. What may have been satisfying to his incensed psyche I will never know. As for me, foul shame penetrated my very soul. I felt dirty and humiliated, utterly defeated. *Polluted*, that ancient Roman term of judgment seeping through the centuries into my pathetic sniffles. I slunk to the bathroom, locking the door, not able to turn toward the mirror. In those minutes while the hot water ran in the tub, I vowed it would never happen again. *One flesh* had become unalterably severed.

John is reading *The New Yorker* and doing crossword puzzles close by as I now write. Knowing I'm recounting this ordeal and writing it out, he just asked me, "Is this hard for you? Is it painful for you to tell of that incident?" My answer was no, as it never could have been before yesterday when I read Shakespeare's "The Rape of Lucrece." I quoted to John, with passion, those memorable lines of a raped woman: *Go get me hither paper, ink, and pen.*

I am writing this chapter on rape during Valentine's Day week 2015, the opening week of the film *Fifty Shades of Grey*. It would have been too easy in the previous chapter on cultural considerations to have made a rant about this film alongside my rant on rap music. But one more old lady whining does little to alleviate the problem. Does the film demean women and celebrate rape? Does it have anything to say on the subject of multinational rape and sex trafficking? You bet it does, at least according to Mimi Haddad, who is the president of Christians for Biblical Equality.

As the film industry promotes *Fifty Shades of Grey*, launching on Valentine's Day, I sit beside sixty scholars, activists, and faith leaders from more than twenty countries at a forum convened by the Carter Center: "Beyond Violence: Women Leading for Peaceful Societies." Working to end the domination of women worldwide, these leaders recognize that "prejudice, discrimination, war, violence, distorted interpretations of religious texts,

physical and mental abuse, poverty, and disease fall dispropor-
tionately on women and girls," as Jimmy Carter notes in *Call to
Action: Women, Religion, Violence, and Power* . . .

While these activists labor to combat abuse, filmmakers
are working to normalize the sexual domination of women as
entertainment . . .

Meanwhile, in hidden corners of nearly every city of the
world, girls and women are held in secret prisons and brothels
where they endure gang-rape. Firearms and other weapons are
used as instruments of rape.[7]

The response of those who defend books and movies like *Fifty
Shades of Grey* is that no one is forced to read the book or watch the
movie, and the kind of sex that is portrayed is assumed to be a choice
that is freely made, not coerced. And what about rape itself? Is that
an act that is a choice freely made by both partners? It obviously is not
rape if it is—*or is it?*

Dare we ask Todd Akin's question: Is a particular incident a case
of "legitimate rape"? I may be walking on thin ice here, but perhaps
the question has merit. As we've already seen when it comes to domestic violence, we should not automatically believe everyone's story. Is
there a motive for someone to lie, perhaps in a child custody battle?
And what is the definition of abuse? Is it abuse when a husband tells
a wife she ought to lose twenty pounds and wear sexy nighties? While
such behavior may not be appropriate, we dare not flatten a crime so
much that it means nothing. If almost *everything* is abuse, then *nothing* is abuse. So it is with rape. If we define it too broadly, the term
almost becomes meaningless. So, then, what is *legitimate rape*?

Let's say one of my seminary students had made a serious commitment to forgo sexual intimacies before marriage. He is dating a
young woman from the college across the way. Let's say she is not a
virgin and does not hold to his high standards. They've been dating
for some time and are getting serious. She's leading him on, maybe
even imagining that sex will seal their relationship. He believes that

premarital sex is a sin and insists they are going too far. He says no. She doesn't stop. He is stronger than she and could push her away and get out of the car and take a long walk. He just keeps saying no. She persists until, against his conscience and better judgment, he succumbs to temptation. Is *she* guilty of rape?

What if the situation is reversed, and she is the one saying no, insisting he is going too far? She says no, telling him to stop. But she does not kick and push and scream and scratch his face with her fingernails. She succumbs. Is *he* guilty of rape?

Does an awful experience in my own marriage fit the definition of rape? These are not easy questions, but they ought to cause us to think deeply about definitions, as well as about contributing factors. For example, did a belief (religious or otherwise) in male supremacy influence the outcome of the sexual encounter? Did corporate power make a difference, let's say, causing a young man on the make in the corporate world to succumb to the demands of his boss? Was he caught off guard, as was Joseph when Potiphar's wife tried to force him into bed?

What is rape? The Bible does not even suggest there is such a category as marital rape. Augustine had strong words, but not relating to the marriage bed. Sir Matthew Hale, a seventeenth-century English jurist, established the legal tradition in the English-speaking world for nonrecognition of rape in marriage. His reasoning was that when women married, they gave themselves to their husbands in a binding contract: "The husband cannot be guilty of a rape committed by himself upon his lawful wife, for by their mutual matrimonial consent and contract the wife hath given herself in this kind unto her husband, which she cannot retract."[8]

Giving license for marital rape, however, is not something out of the dark past. Until the 1970s, there were no laws in the United States making marital rape a crime. And even today noncriminalization of marital rape has its supporters. Virginia state senator Richard Black, in 2002, asked his fellow assemblymen "how on earth you could validly get a conviction of a husband-wife rape when they're living together, sleeping in the same bed, she's in a nightie, and so forth, there's no injury, there's no separation or anything."[9]

But if we assume this subject is a matter that interests only lawmakers, we are mistaken. In the summer of 2012, a lengthy quote by megachurch minister Doug Wilson was posted on the website of the Gospel Coalition, whose council members include Tim Keller, Al Mohler, and John Piper. "We have forgotten the biblical concepts of true authority and submission, or more accurately, have rebelled against them," writes Wilson. "However we try, the sexual act cannot be made into an egalitarian pleasuring party. A man penetrates, conquers, colonizes, plants. A woman receives, surrenders, accepts."

Aware that this may seem shocking, he blames the "rebels": "This is, of course, offensive to all egalitarians, and so our culture has rebelled against the concept of authority and submission in marriage . . . as they relate to the marriage bed."[10]

Authority and submission were key factors in the awful nightmare I experienced. But I continue to mull over the question, *Did I endure a legitimate marital rape?* For anyone who might have a prurient interest in exactly what happened, there would be real disappointment even if I were to describe it in minute detail, which fortunately I have mostly erased from my memory. Prior to the incident, I had made journal entries that bear on the issue.

January 22, 1986

Sexual submission, as he defines it, has not related to my unwillingness to have intercourse with him. I have very rarely denied him that ... My lack of submission is rather my "pulling away" from him at night. That charge is partially true. His fixation with anal touching has bothered me, as have other things he's tried to do. I woke up early one morning to discover him on his knees on his side of the bed with a flashlight under the covers looking at my rectal area. I have also caught him peeking through the keyhole while I was in the bathroom.

August 11, 1987

Today begins the 20th year of our marriage. Yesterday was our anniversary, but there was no mention of it from [him]—not from me either. I guess that was appropriate. How can you celebrate or even acknowledge something that is so torn apart as our marriage—except, of course, that [he] still expects and gets sex. If our marriage is good enough for that, I guess I would think that it would be good enough for him to suggest we go out to eat at a nice restaurant on our 19th anniversary, but if we haven't gone out in the previous 18 years, why start now.

There are many reasons that the term *rape* is less than appropriate and exact in my case. I have read and listened to horrific accounts of rape, and thus I wonder if I should actually use the term. I did not kick or scream when my ex-husband demanded sex, but I let him know how utterly disgusting I found his demand to be. There was nothing remotely mutual about the encounter. I was forced to have sex with my ex-husband. Or was I? When I look back on that ugly ordeal, I struggle even to this day to actually place myself amid that utterly repulsive scene, though truly I was there.

She is in her forties, a strong capable woman, albeit a wife who had been beaten and battered and pummeled and terrorized on many occasions by her husband. So one morning, she is packing her bags to make a car trip to speak at long-scheduled meetings. The husband enters the bedroom, his mood dark and foreboding. And then the threat. There is no physical violence this time, but the demand for sex—sex or stay home. No alternative. She would not be leaving the bedroom or the house until she had submitted to sex. He, as he had told their minister, and had reminded her on many occasions, was the "head of the home from the bedroom to the kitchen."

What was I to do? Should I have grabbed the phone and tried to call 911? Phones had been broken over similar issues before. And the police? Even if I had been able to make such a call, it would have been laughable to report that my husband is ordering me to have sex before leaving town. The story probably would have made one of those lists of the silliest police reports. I suppose I could have tried to put through a call (had my ex-husband permitted) to someone in charge of the meetings and simply told the truth or made up a lie that I was sick. What were my choices? Do I succumb to the demeaning act of nonconsensual sex, fulfill my obligations, contact an attorney when I arrive back home, and file for separate maintenance?

Was this an incident of *legitimate* rape? And was it even the worst incident of sexual abuse I had suffered? Whether *legitimate* or not, the rape I experienced was considerably less vile and spiteful than other of his sexual violations against me. Before I went to court to plead for separate maintenance and full custody of Carlton, my attorney recorded on his yellow pad my testimony of abuse. My journal was helpful, but he insisted on more details. I resisted, embarrassed to reveal some of the utterly icky incidents. He pressed, and I felt forced to tell him of a revulsion I had never before voiced. I begged him not to ask me about it in court. He said it would depend on his discernment of the mind-set of the judge. He had already told me I had been assigned the judge he least desired for my case.

So there I was in court, testifying to shameful episodes, prompted by my lawyer. Fortunately the room was empty except for the judge, two attorneys, and a court recorder. My ex-husband, living out of state, did not make a showing. With my testimony over, we took a brief recess before Carlton was scheduled to enter the courtroom to testify. In the restroom, I came face-to-face with the court recorder. Perhaps she spoke out of turn. Her words tumbled out. "I'm so sorry about what you've endured. In all my years in court, I've never recorded such disgusting abuse. I hope everything works out." Her only words. When I returned after recess, she was in her place, her demeanor that of a robot back to recording.

And my testimony in court was not the worst of it. (A reminder that everything in this chapter and nearly all of the domestic violence detailed in this book occurred in the years after we moved from Crown Point to Grand Rapids—in the years after I did not report my ex-husband's sexual abuse of Deana. The sordid stories I did not fully detail in court relate to a trip out west and four weeks of camping in the summer of 1985. If I were to write of these episodes in this manuscript, I would delete the paragraph before it was finished. I have no such delete capabilities to erase memory.

These reprehensible acts that occurred during my first marriage could in no way—not even remotely—be characterized in terms of love or mutuality.

Some eight months before I escaped my domestic dungeon of violence, the *Grand Rapids Press* (February 24, 1987) carried an Associated Press story: "Michigan's rape law, which forbids anyone from being charged with raping their spouse, is being studied for possible change following a ruling that freed a man convicted of raping his estranged wife."

I found that clipped article recently while sorting through my files. Had I taken any consolation at the time the law was being studied? I seriously doubt it. Here was a man, now free, who had raped his estranged wife. Who could possibly understand or care about my situation? I was not yet estranged from my husband, and I could barely make a case for *legitimate* rape.

Longtime former editor of *Charisma* magazine Lee Grady wrote about the dark side of wives submitting to their husbands. Many of his stories are about women he encountered in his worldwide travels. A woman in Hungary confided that her husband, a professing Christian, forced her to "engage in sexual acts with him that made her feel uncomfortable and dirty." He talked with women in Kenya who told him their "AIDS-infected husbands often raped them—and then their pastors told them they must submit." And in America, he has counseled "women [who] are told that obedience to God is measured by their wifely submission—even if their husbands are addicted to alcohol or pornography or if they are involved in adulterous affairs."

Grady stands out among evangelicals. He has called out his fellow church leaders on this subject. "This distortion of biblical teaching has plunged countless Christian women into depression and emotional trauma," he writes. "I'm not sure which is worse: the harsh words they hear from their husbands or the perverse way the Bible is wielded as a leather belt to justify domestic abuse."[11]

In many ways, it seems to be a strange coincidence that I am writing this chapter on rape in the middle of February 2015. The weekend began with Friday the 13th, the very day that almost everyone, it seemed, was hurrying to the theaters for the Valentines weekend blockbuster *Fifty Shades of Grey*.

As I contemplate these clanging symbols, I wonder if the best antidote to *fifty shades of rape* is to quote in full one of the most touching love letters I've ever read. John doesn't write love letters, so I have to read mine vicariously—in this case from the pen of David Martyn Lloyd-Jones (1899–1981). He was the much-celebrated minister of Westminster Chapel in London, succeeding G. Campbell Morgan. Martyn was also a widely read author and onetime president of InterVarsity Fellowship (UK). He is revered today by New Calvinists for his strong endorsement of Calvinism during the mid-twentieth century.

His engagement and subsequent marriage in 1927 is what I find most interesting. Martyn was a medical doctor, and Bethan Phillips had only recently passed her exams at the University College Hospital in London, which certified her to practice medicine as well. But then a chance meeting on a tennis court turned their lives upside down. They fell in love and married. But within a month after their marriage, having given up their medical careers, they found themselves serving in a run-down city mission. "So began eleven-and-a-half happy, fruitful years, for which I will always thank God," she wrote fifty years later.[12]

She was a brilliant and confident woman. They both had given up careers for what they believed was a higher calling. His letter to her, written in early autumn 1939, needs no introductory comment except to point out that it is a monument to a marriage of mutuality.

My dear Bethan,

Thank you for your letter of this morning, though I am very angry that you should have been up till 11:30 p.m. writing it! . . . As I have told you many, many times, the passing of the years does nothing but deepen and intensify my love for you. When I think of those days in London in 1925 and '26, when I thought that no greater love was possible, I could laugh . . .

I am quite certain that there is no lover, anywhere, writing to his girl who is quite as mad about her as I am. Indeed I pity those lovers who are not married. Well, I had better put a curb on things or I shall spend the night writing to you . . .

Ever yours—Martyn[13]

10

risky or reliable?

Couples Counseling for Domestic Violence

I take no joy in being a whistle blower, but it's time. I am a committed marriage and family therapist, having practiced this form of therapy since 1977. I train marriage and family therapists. I believe that marriage therapy can be very helpful in the hands of therapists who are committed to the profession and the practice. But there are a lot of problems out there with the practice of therapy—a lot of problems.

WILLIAM J. DOHERTY, PHD

October 16, 1987. The national news was the stock market. Three days later, all fears came to fruition on Black Monday 1987. The Dow dropped 508 points. Though I had no money invested, I was deeply concerned for friends and for the nation itself. Indeed, it was a very scary time.

But for me, the day was Freedom Friday, though hardly freedom without dread of what would happen next. Yet for a few short hours, Carlton and I were convinced the terror of the past years had finally come to an end.

We had been secretly planning and preparing for weeks. His clothes, shoes, and other necessities had been boxed and hidden in his closet. I had done the same, gathering papers, books, clothes, and everything I would need for an extended time away from home. More than a month earlier, I had visited the Grand Rapids Domestic Crisis Center, filled out a long form, and waited for a social worker to look it over before she called me in for a consultation.

The center had housing available for poor women and their children who were escaping violence in the home. I qualified. I was poor and lived with my son in a violent setting. But the social worker saw things differently. I was dressed in my adjunct professor garb. Not a good choice. Worse than that, however, was the required information form—particularly the question asking about my education and the highest degree I had been awarded. She looked at me skeptically. "You have a PhD?"

"Yes," I told her.

"This is not the place for you. You need to talk with someone at the Women's Resource Center. They can give you professional help."

I protested. "I already talked with them," I explained. "They sent me here because I need a place to go for a week or so until the court makes a decision."

The Domestic Crisis Center in Grand Rapids turned its back on my domestic crisis.

If I could not find help from the Domestic Crisis Center, where else could I go? I was a member of a church only three miles from my home. I had previously talked with our senior pastor, who had been aware of my husband's anger issues, but he was very hesitant about getting involved. He had agreed to meet with my husband on one occasion, but later he told me that my husband had spent the entire time defending male headship. My ex-husband also told the pastor that the problems in the marriage were mine—that he was the rightful head of the home "from the kitchen to the bedroom." Our pastor realized he did not have the tools to mediate our very serious marital problems. At least he didn't tell me to go home and submit—like many ministers do. His concern was for my welfare.

In the end, the church took me in. Why hadn't I gone there in the first place? Like so many women, I was terribly ashamed. To ask for help was much easier when the woman behind the desk was a stranger. But I was forced to swallow my pride. And then we were welcomed with open arms into the home of our associate pastor, Dick Doeden, and his wife, Nancy. More than that, Dick took Carlton under his wing during the two weeks we stayed with them—including sending him out to the big backyard to rake leaves. A mother couldn't ask for more. And in the weeks after we left their home, Dick would call and ask if Carlton could join him at a few Hope College football games.

After a temporary court settlement, Carlton and I returned to our home the day after my ex-husband was ordered to move out. My abuser was at least temporarily out of the picture, and we weren't talking to each other.

"Forced counseling never works." That was the response of the psychologist on the other end of the line after I had summarized my situation. ("He's the best counselor in town," I had been told.) "If a spouse agrees to counseling under the threat of divorce," he told me, "don't even bother trying to drag him in. It never works."

We had not gone to counseling prior to that fateful day of separation two weeks earlier. Carlton had caught a ride to school in the morning with his dad, who was on his way to work. As I had arranged with his school, he was permitted to return home as soon as it was safe. Within minutes, he raced through the front door and went upstairs to get the boxes we had packed and hidden. We filled the van and got away before noon, fearing his father might just decide to stop home at midday.

After unloading at the Doedens' home, we headed for a meat market and bought bones, sneaked back into our house, and left them in the refrigerator for Rafiki, our dog. Next stop, the grocery store, where we bought a roasted chicken and fixings and headed out of town. We found a two-track road in a wooded area overlooking a horse pasture. It was an absolutely beautiful autumn setting. We parked and opened the doors of our old Westfalia van for the best meal we'd ever eaten. I'll never forget Carlton's comment as we set the table: "Finally, we're free." Today, more than a quarter century later, we remind each other of those moments of freedom we shared together.

My escaping with Carlton, however, was anything but the tranquil loveliness of an autumn horse farm. The fear that both of us felt when "we separated from Dad," as he has always termed it, was very real. *Would he kill me?* He would go to prison, of course. But what would happen to Carlton?

No counseling could have alleviated my fears—fears based on knowledge, not paranoia. But I did in a most mysterious way benefit from counseling—from arms that enfolded me in the night, as though God had somehow reached down through the light-years and touched me. The night before Carlton and I made our escape, I had gone out walking, alone as I often did, Rafiki on a leash. A few blocks from home, I noticed two women coming toward me—one black, one white. They greeted me under a lamppost and we had a few pleasant remarks, and then the black woman said something I might have construed as inappropriate. It was dark. They could hardly see me. She said, "You look troubled." I began to say I was doing fine, but I choked. The words refused to form. They both put their arms around me as I sobbed. When I got my voice back, I told them briefly about the situation. They prayed for me there in the dark. They held on and didn't want to let me go, promising to remember to pray for me. I never saw them again. *Maybe it was a vision*, I sometimes think. But I know, whenever I recall those moments on that dark street, I was visited by God that night. I'm reminded of the words of Cardinal John

Henry Newman's hymn, "Lead, kindly Light, amid th' encircling gloom, lead thou me on."

I did not know how I would navigate the months and years ahead as a single mother. Having filed for separate maintenance, not divorce, I had no intention of ever remarrying. Financially, Carlton and I struggled. He picked up odd jobs and held down two paper routes while staying active in sports—sometimes convincing his mother to sub on his paper route. In fact, I became adept at delivering the *Grand Rapids Press* and may have been the best seminary professor ever to carry out that job. But bills piled up, and I ended up borrowing money from my thirteen-year-old son to make ends meet.

For our first Thanksgiving on our own, we invited my sister Kathy from Madison, Wisconsin. We had turkey and all the fixings, though dealing with that aspect of the holiday had proven to be very difficult.

A few days earlier, I had greeted Pastor Dick at the door. He had two large bags in his arms. It was a gesture of kindness on behalf of the church, and I graciously thanked him for the thoughtfulness. When he left, I cringed in shame at what had just happened. I had been the one who had helped in past years with such handouts, and now I was on the receiving end.

But I pulled myself together, and by the time Carlton arrived home from school, I was able to say in a cheery voice that Dick had brought over a turkey and much more. But before I could finish the sentence, Carlton was howling. "Why did you take it?" His outrage was worse than I could have anticipated. "You could have just said no."

I told him I had no choice. He screamed back that I *did* have a choice, that I should have said no, that people would find out. "Why did you do it?" he screamed. "Now everyone will know. Don't you care about me and about how I feel?"

I did care. I knew when I accepted the gift that I was paying for it with the gall of my own shame and even more with Carlton's shame. But there was no alternative. I had to show gratitude and accept the gift.

In the months that followed, tension increased between Carlton and me. In many ways, our situation was not healthy. He would go through the stack of bills and figure out what he would have to earn to pay them if a health problem were to set me aside. He could pick up more odd jobs and make it. He was stepping in as the man of the house. But he was a thirteen-year-old kid, and I was a strict and protective mother. Both strong-willed, we clashed. Finally things got so bad, I contacted a counseling clinic and set up an appointment. I went to several sessions but seemed to be making little progress with a therapist who had never been married or had children herself. She did say it was imperative for her to meet with Carlton and me together.

Not surprisingly, he was defiant. There was no way I was going to drag him into counseling. I put my foot down, and he came along. It was not a pleasant session, as he sulked most of the time. Little, if anything, was accomplished. We walked out of the brick building into a sunny spring day. Neither of us spoke. As we got to the car, he couldn't hold back his contempt any longer. "Why do you waste your money on her? She's crazier than you are." He was right. She *was* crazier than I was. I went back for one more session, paid my final bill, and left therapy behind.

From then on, our relationship improved. School was out a few weeks later, and through my frugality, we were able to travel the roads of Michigan and splurge on mini-vacations. We got up early on Sunday mornings. I drove the car and folded papers while he delivered. Then off to church and on the road, not needing to return until paper delivery time late on Monday afternoon. Those are memories we'll carry for the rest of our lives.

The counseling that served me best in the months that followed my escape with Carlton and our return home came by way of informal encouragement from family, friends, and colleagues. The shame I felt in revealing the violence of my ex-husband to my siblings was overturned in direct proportion to their showering Carlton and me with love and concern. Older brother David and his wife, Sharon, sent a lovely arrangement of flowers that arrived only days after we had escaped. Younger brother Jonnie demanded to know if I needed financial help. Whatever we needed (or didn't need) would be sent immediately. His offer showed pure concern for our well-being, not a hint of obligation. My sisters were equally supportive.

Dozens of people almost seemed to materialize out of nowhere, simply offering care and kindness. But the ones whose words meant the most were my longtime colleagues at Trinity. They could have avoided the subject after President Meyer briefly filled them in at a faculty meeting. I was not there and do not know what he said, but the outpouring of concern and support overwhelmed me. And particularly from those on the opposite side of "the women's issue." During my seventeen years at Trinity, that topic was a hot button, and I was on the "liberal" side in the eyes of many of my colleagues. But differences of opinion counted for nothing when I was hurting.

So it was that for me the most effective counseling came in informal settings. And my case was certainly not weakened by the fact that my ex-husband had left a trail of deceit and dishonesty. Many people commented to me that they had been aware of previous situations but had refrained from saying anything to me about it. So much for my capabilities as the queen of cover-up.

I look back with indignation at the actual "marriage counseling" I endured. After separating from my ex-husband, I still believed I should press him to participate in counseling. He refused to go to a certified counselor, and finally I conceded to go to a Bible church minister whose church was some twenty miles north of Grand Rapids, where no one would know us. As I reflect back, I am truly bewildered as to what was going through my mind. Carlton and I were free at last. Why would I even consider subjecting him to having his father back in the home? And why would I not demand a professional? When my ex-husband refused, I should have said *adios*. I didn't. I was bound and determined to give things one last try—perhaps to assuage my own feelings of guilt, if nothing else.

Had I read what is available from so many sources today in books and in articles online, I'm convinced I would not have spent my time and money with this incompetent small-church minister (though I certainly don't want to imply that a megachurch minister would have served more competently in our situation).

"Couples counseling or marriage counseling is never an appropriate strategy to address abusive behavior—especially domestic violence," writes Terry Moore, a licensed clinical addiction counselor. "Resolving the kind of conflicts between people for which couples counseling is intended will not stop one person from abusing the other. Conflict is a pretext for abuse, not a cause of it."[1] Having since read up on the subject, these statements sound so obvious. Why wouldn't I as a smart, educated woman have recognized these truths to be self-evident—for my own declaration of independence?

What Moore writes is so elementary and obvious that I'm almost embarrassed to quote it: "Couples counseling depends upon an open dialogue between partners . . . People who are being hit, intimidated, or controlled through threats or other coercive means by their partners are not free to engage in an open dialogue." But I wasn't the only one back then, and even today, who was entirely clueless on this critical matter.

Moore emphasizes that before an abuser even undergoes couples counseling, it is imperative that he enter a certified Batterers Intervention Program (BIP). But even BIPs are only as effective as the abuser's commitment to turn his life around. Ray Rice had been through anger management courses before beating his fiancée. So even BIP is no cure-all.

Who is this Terry Moore? I didn't know if she might be a woman. I've known women whose name was spelled that way. But Terry, as it turns out, is a man, pictured on his website with a beard and in a baseball cap, smiling but appearing tough enough to take on a violent husband, no ball bat needed. He is an expert on domestic violence who is often interviewed on TV and in other media and was featured in the 2003 nationally award-winning documentary *Journeys of Survival: Indianapolis Responds to Domestic Abuse.*

I knew nothing about Terry or the likes of him when I was contemplating marriage counseling. Not only had my ex-husband not agreed to anything comparable to BIP, but he also refused to go to a certified counselor because he was convinced that such a therapist might agree with me and thus usurp his headship. That I did not recognize this as a giant red flag blowing in the Michigan icy winter will always stump me.

My ex-husband and I were together for our first meeting with the Bible church minister. The minister offered a prayer and then asked me, since I had initiated the counseling, to explain the problem. I briefly recounted many incidents of my husband breaking down doors, beating me, and threatening to kill me. Besides this cursory summary, I might have referred to one of my recent journal entries:

September 19, 1986

I discovered that all our financial files were missing from the
file drawer where they have been kept for years. I asked [him]
about it. He said I had no reason to have access to them since he
kept the finances in the family.

Or I might have read aloud a much more descriptive entry on violence that I had written exactly one month before the previous entry. I didn't. But if I had, I cannot imagine it would have made any difference.

August 19, 1986

Last night was a terrible ordeal . . . We were in the process of
drilling holes for insulating my study when I brought up the
subject of my book (which I obviously shouldn't have done at
that time). He went out of control, threw the drill on the floor,
knocked me to the floor, and broke the latch on the bathroom
door by slamming it so hard. He yelled and screamed for most
of an hour, refusing to allow me to work on the room or leave.
I remained relatively calm . . . When we were downstairs, he

*grabbed me by the arm, squeezing as hard as he could, and
stomped on my bare foot (I'm black-and-blue today as a result),
and he would have done more had Carlton not come and
screamed at him to stop.*

The minister then turned to my husband, himself an ordained
Bible church minister. What could he possibly say in the face of such
accusations? I expected him to show anger and call me a liar, as he
had done so often previously (a term, by the way, I had never used of
him). I had expected him to say I was making up stories—that he had
never beaten me or threatened to kill me. Lies. Lies. Lies. Rather, he
calmly spoke of my disobedience. His focus was on my refusal to leave
Fifth Reformed Church, a "liberal" church where we both had been
members. Perhaps he assumed he was scoring points with this minister, himself part of the Independent Fundamentalist Churches of
America (IFCA). When the minister asked in what ways the church
was liberal, my husband carried on for ten minutes about the anthems
the choir was now singing, as though anthems by their very nature
were liberal.

Appearing a bit confused, the minister went on to his marriage
counseling script. He turned to Ephesians 5 in his Bible and read how
wives must submit to their husbands, and how husbands must love
their wives. He then reached over to his desk for two small pieces of
paper, each one having appropriate Bible verses for us to reflect on.
He concluded by arranging to meet with us separately the following
week. That was it. My husband stayed behind as I walked out in the
cold December wind to the heaterless, broken-down van I had gotten
in the separation agreement. I wadded up the little paper the minister
had given me, stuck it in my coat pocket, and never looked at it again.

When I returned the following week, I had three pages of mate-
rial for the minister relating to my ex-husband's domestic abuse,
arrests, job firings, and child sexual abuse. I asked the minister to
read them aloud while I followed along on my own copy. He did, and

we discussed some of the charges. He said he would speak to my husband about those issues. But his only real concern for me was that we discuss the verses he had given me on wifely submission. I argued that I had already gone way too far in so-called "submission" by not reporting crimes—particularly a crime he had committed against a young girl. He responded that a wife's first loyalty was not to the legal system but to Christ—and to Christ by way of submission to her husband.

The winter sessions, which were more than I could afford and too far to drive with a vehicle with no heat, lasted for several more weeks before I simply informed the minister in January that I would be unable to continue. Yet I felt guilty about dropping out. Then some months later, I ran into a longtime acquaintance who had become aware of my situation. She piled on guilt in the other direction. "Codependency is your problem," she insisted. "You need to find a good counselor who can do some in-depth codependency therapy with you. You'll never heal until you have gone through an intensive program." I was too poor and too busy, but she wouldn't get off my case until I refused to talk with her further.

And then another woman studying psychology at Fuller Seminary heard about my situation. I was teaching a summer course at the school in Pasadena, and Carlton came along to work at odd jobs. She sought me out and wanted to subject me to her free therapy. She was a smart student near graduation, highly respected by several faculty members, so I took the bait. She analyzed me quickly. My problem: I was in denial. Although she didn't say it, she implied that I was *hopelessly* in denial.

By this time, I was gaining my own voice when it came to therapy, essentially acceding to Carlton's assessment that the therapist was crazier than I was. My response to this well-meaning, about-to-graduate therapist was to respond to her diagnosis that I was in denial with a firm "Yes! That is the only way I survive." Indeed, how does any single mother raise a strong-minded teenage son without a good dose of denial?

And I was also in denial about the terrible violence and abuse in my marriage. The journals I had written were set aside. I was on the road with my dear friend Paul, not considering myself *healed*, but *forgetting what was behind* me during those difficult years and *reaching out for what was ahead, I pressed on toward the goal.* Paul, in Philippians 3, was seeking "to win the prize for which God has called [him] heavenward in Christ Jesus." For me, my goal at the time was often no more than to get through another day without drama with an impetuous son and to cherish each exhilarating moment we were able to enjoy together.

Did I need therapy? Do all individuals who endure domestic abuse need therapy? For me, getting out of the situation was incredible relief enough. *Forgetting what was behind* was exactly what I needed.

For some people, therapy may be exactly what is needed. But not all patients heal the same way. I was reminded of that recently when two people close to me had a similar hernia surgery, both being told it would take at least six weeks to begin to really feel healed. One was up and about and off meds in a few days and raring to go; the other, much younger, was laid up for two weeks. The one for whom the pain was more serious should not be criticized for needing the extra rest and meds. The same is true for those who have endured psychological trauma. We should not judge those who require more or less *doctoring*. Our bodies and minds and emotions and psyches heal differently.

But if I managed to survive without a lot of doctoring, I often wonder how women manage to survive the doctoring accompanied by bad advice. I truly do not believe this happens intentionally. Rather such doctoring is given by those who truly believe it is the best medicine. I put John Piper's counsel in this category. He writes:

> Several years ago, I was asked in an online Q&A, "What should a wife's submission to her husband look like if he's an abuser?"
>
> One of the criticisms of my answer has been that I did not mention the recourse that a wife has to law enforcement for protection. So let me clarify with seven biblical considerations.[2]

As others have pointed out, Piper's confession ominously suggests that for several years, any wife following his advice would not have sought out law enforcement. In his lengthy clarification, he does not apologize to any woman who may have been gravely harmed by that oversight. Here is a representative piece of his clarification:

> A wife's submission to the authority of civil law, for Christ's sake, may, therefore, overrule her submission to a husband's demand that she endure his injuries. This legitimate recourse to civil protection may be done in a spirit that does not contradict the spirit of love and submission to her husband, for a wife may take this recourse with a heavy and humble heart that longs for her husband's repentance and the restoration of his nurturing leadership.[3]

I often wish that John Piper, author of the bestselling book *Desiring God*, would not share so much online. I like him. He's actually a very kind individual. But it seems he almost sets himself up for criticism. Indeed, there is something terribly wrong in even his clarification. He is asserting that a husband who demands that his wife "endure his injuries" is still the rightful head in the marriage. She must be submissive to him unless the authority of civil [not criminal] law overrules. How does civil law *overrule* without a court case? How does a wife seek civil protection and at the same time make sure "it does not contradict the spirit of love and submission to her husband"?

It's almost as though Piper is living in a parallel universe. He just doesn't seem to get it. Does he have any understanding at all of the law or of tyrannical husbands? The only civil protection a wife can obtain in such circumstances is a restraining order, and until the matter goes to court, she would be expected to flee the dangerous home. There is no such thing as "civil protection" that arrives at the beck and call of a beaten wife and hangs around her home to protect her. And let's not be naive. Is the abusive husband really going to give her permission to leave him and perhaps take the children with her? The scenario has no relevance to the real world and carries dangerous implications.

Of course, Piper is not alone in this kind of counseling of women who experience domestic violence. What if a woman is seeking help at Rick Warren's Saddleback Church? A temporary separation and marriage counseling are the answers. The standard for separation, however, is that the abuser has the "habit of beating you regularly." Such counsel does not come from a woman who has suffered domestic violence. This is the advice from teaching pastor Tom Holladay. "How many beatings would have to take place in order to qualify as *regularly*?" asks Jocelyn Andersen, a domestic violence survivor and the author of *Woman Submit! Christians and Domestic Violence*.[4] Too often, the counsel women receive is as dangerous as the abuse itself, subjecting them to a submissive role in the face of violence.

But what about the value of marriage counseling for couples who are embroiled in very serious conflict where there is no physical violence? Here is not the place for a marriage manual or even advice on how married couples should work things out, though my final chapter in this book is largely devoted to how issues have been dealt with by one couple, namely, John and me. But how might my previous marriage have been saved had my husband not beaten and terrorized me? Is it possible, for example, for a strong egalitarian and an equally strong complementarian to live happily together as husband and wife?

I'm not a counselor, though my students have often asked me for advice and occasionally for long-term mentoring. I consider myself a good listener and a good questioner, but I've rarely served in this capacity for more than a session. If I were to hang out a shingle, it would simply read, "Dr. Ruth," and I would most certainly charge more for my services than Lucy's five cents, per the *Peanuts* comic strip.

The advice I typically gave my students was by way of recommending a book, most often a biography. A student came to me once, having been raped some years earlier. A professional therapist had not helped. I suggested a biography of Helen Roseveare, a missionary who had been repeatedly raped during the Simba Rebellion in the

Congo—a woman who had come to terms with the terrible violence. My student found the book very helpful.

The book I would recommend to married couples who have strong differences of opinion on major issues is one I have just finished: *Love and War: Twenty Years, Three Presidents, Two Daughters, and One Louisiana Home* by Mary Matalin and James Carville.[5] As a halfhearted political junkie, I have been fascinated by their politics and their relationship for more than two decades. He was considered the brains behind the Bill Clinton presidential election in 1992, and she held a similar campaign position on the opposing side for the reelection of George H. W. Bush.

How have they managed to live in harmony for more than two decades? Actually, they have not, and the book details very difficult periods—some that lasted for months. Their problems related not only to serious differences in politics but also to personality differences. He, the *liberal* Democrat, operates on strict rules and schedules with absolutely no tolerance for her "yak-a-thons" with friends that sometimes extend into the wee hours of the morning. She's a spender; he's a saver. Observers find this more than a little humorous, since the favorite Republican accusation against Democrats is that they are big spenders.

Yet despite the differences, their marriage was based on mutuality. And they vowed "till death do us part." In fact, they tell of getting married three times—their first being a New Orleans civil marriage complete with a Mardi Gras "dancin' in the street" atmosphere. They emphasize, however, that their marriage was anything but a stunt, as some reporters had suggested. The second was a surprise tenth-anniversary wedding that James had secretly planned, with oldest daughter Mattie, then eight, performing the ceremony. When she got to the point in the script calling for words "with the power vested in me," she stopped and with a confused shake of her head innocently said, "I don't have any power." This was the most memorable line at wedding number two. The third wedding was a small, serious affair conducted by a priest after Mary had joyously converted to Catholicism. James considers himself a "cafeteria Catholic" who argues endlessly with the monsignor. Mary, the convert, takes her faith much more seriously. Both of them, however, take the vows of their marriage with extraordinary seriousness.

This is a book I would gladly give to any couple who is contemplating the abandonment of their wedding vows and filing for divorce. Mary and James demonstrate not only how a couple can rise above serious differences but also how they were able to put things in place that brought them closer together. A complementarian marriage model would not have worked. Even if James had shown loving headship and had very kindly informed Mary that she must submit to him and follow him into Democratic political activism, it would have only exacerbated the situation. She would no more support Democrats than I would have supported George Wallace at my husband's command in 1968.

Their decision to move from Washington, D.C., to New Orleans and to gradually move away from direct involvement in partisan politics was a major turn toward marital harmony. Finding common ground was critical. Together they began working with both Democrats and Republicans in rebuilding New Orleans after the devastation of Hurricane Katrina. Toxic differences abated as their abiding love and laughter held firm.

In a December 2009 interview on CNN's *State of the Union*, host John King invited questions about how James and Mary managed to stay married. An Indiana resident texted in this question: "Can you show both houses of Congress your secret for compromise?" Mary responded: "Well, we're not a democracy. We're an enlightened MOM-archy. That's what we are."

James, trying to get a word in edgewise, summed up their mutuality: "I don't have a position on anything domestically. So I just say yes, and then go on and do it. I mean it. I would say the three ingredients to successful marriage are surrender, capitulation, and retreat. If you've got those three things—."[6] Laughter quelled his final words.

From the bottom of my heart,
Mary and James,
I wish you well.
Yes, till death do you part.

11

two to tango?

The Burden of Shame, Blame, and Guilt

Rescuing women from their burden of unwarranted guilt is going to require "educational practices and socializing agents" even more effective than the ones that have been relentlessly loading female humans with responsibility for other people's behavior from their earliest childhood.

GERMAINE GREER

I wonder if she was contentious." That was the comment a colleague posed after David Duyst was charged with killing his wife, Sandy. Several of us were sitting around a table in the faculty room eating our lunch. "Contentious?" I looked at him in disbelief. "Well," he responded, "you have to wonder what she might have done. It takes two to tango, you know." Others (all male) then jumped into the discussion.

Having already finished my lunch, I went on my way. I was upset, and I didn't want to deal with the matter in front of all my colleagues. Never mind that David, as was proved at the trial, was having an affair and had just taken out a large life insurance policy on Sandy. *It takes two to tango.* Never mind that she had been shot *twice* in the back of the head, and he insisted it was suicide. (Maybe once, not twice, is the most a person is able to pull that trigger.)

It takes two to tango. Not always. No wife is perfect. Far from it. I certainly wasn't during those nineteen years of marriage. But I pleaded with my husband to go to marriage counseling. He refused. Our problems, he insisted, were all my fault anyway. Besides, marriage counseling, he claimed, by its very nature usurped his headship. A woman certainly is capable of being contentious, indeed, to the point that she's impossible to live with. If Sandy had been such a woman and counseling offered no relief, David had the option of separation or divorce.

It takes two to tango. Bruce Ware, a professor of theology at Southern Baptist Theological Seminary, has asserted that a wife who refuses to submit to her husband is at least in part to blame for the abuse. In many instances, a woman blames herself, convinced that it truly does *take two to tango.* That was true with Meredith Vieira, a correspondent for NBC News and a television talk show host. Her story is told best in her own words:

> I was in an abusive relationship many, many years ago as a young woman . . . It started out, I loved this guy. It started out, we'd have a fight and he'd just sort of grab my arm. I didn't think a lot about it, and then it turned into pushing me into a wall and then it went beyond that, to [his] actually taking his hand and grabbing my face and saying, "I could ruin your career if I wanted to and no one would watch you."[1]

We understand why an evangelical preacher's wife might stay in an abusive relationship, or why a mother of young children who needs a husband's financial support might stay. But why would someone like a successful, single, young news reporter stay in such a relationship? And what does this phenomenon have to do with blame and guilt?

> I'm a smart woman . . . [and heard] a lot of people say, "Well, who would stay in that situation?" Somebody who doesn't have the wherewithal to get out, the means to get out. [But] I had that. I had a job at the time, and I kept in this relationship. I've done a lot of thinking about why, and I think part of it was fear. I was scared of him. I was scared if I tried to leave something worse could happen to me. Part of it was guilt, because every time we would have a fight he would then start crying and say, "I promise I won't do it again," and I would feel like maybe I contributed somehow to this—and they are saying this about Ray Rice's wife, that it takes two to tango.[2]

Then there was a horrific episode. She had endured abuse from the man she loved, but now she was certain he had gone way over the line.

> There was the night, we shared an apartment, and he threw me into a shower, naked with scalding water, and then he threw me outside into the hallway . . . We lived in an apartment building, and I hid in the stairwell for two hours until he came again, crying, "I promise I won't do this again."[3]

So, the next day when he was out of the apartment, she packed her bags and left for good. True or false? False. How could she *not* leave? She didn't have a half dozen kids. She was a young single woman on the make. Unbelievably, she stayed.

> I continued to stay in that relationship until I was offered a job in another state and that's where I felt I had the ability to get away . . . It's not so easy to just get away. You think it would be, but it's not . . . That's just my experience with it, and I know it's rampant in this country, and we all have to accept the fact that it's not just an issue with the NFL—it's an issue with all of our lives, and until we take it seriously, more and more women are going to get abused.[4]

Since 1986, Meredith Vieira has been married to Richard Cohen, and they have three children. Her story is one of those told in Elsa Walsh's *Divided Lives: Public and Private Struggles of Three American Women*.[5] She has been able to move on and navigate the difficulties of life, minus domestic violence.

What is most telling about Vieira's story are her words: "Part of it was guilt, because every time we would have a fight he would then start crying . . . I would feel like maybe I contributed somehow to this—and they are saying this about Ray Rice's wife, that it takes two to tango."

The assumption that it takes two to tango is part of our DNA. From ancient legends to Shakespeare's *The Taming of the Shrew*, we are entertained by women like Katharina, that incorrigible, callous shrew. Even before this time, medieval street dramas featured Noah, who had to beat his disobedient wife to get her away from her gossips and into the ark. But perhaps Charles Dickens did as much as any writer to portray the shrewish wife. He was the most popular British writer of the nineteenth century, and his women are all too often portrayed as evil, as he regarded his own wife. Dickens loved teenage girls, and he had a longtime extramarital relationship with a young woman.

One of the books John read to me recently was Claire Tomalin's *The Invisible Woman: The Story of Nelly Ternan and Charles Dickens*. Nelly was an eighteen-year-old actress, he a larger-than-life, forty-five-year-old entertainer and bestselling writer. In order to justify that affair and others, he denigrated his wife. In a letter to a friend, he wrote, "Catherine is as near being a donkey as one of her sex can be."[6]

Exactly what he meant by calling her a donkey is difficult to say. Accusing her of stupidity would simply not square with who she was—attractive and intelligent, an author in her own right. After bearing ten of his children, however, she no doubt had lost some of her looks and liveliness. He blamed her. He blamed her, not only for being an unfit mother, but also for her frequent pregnancies and the birth of their ten children, as though he was an innocent bystander. He forced her out of their marital home when she was in her early forties, naming her younger, prettier sister as mistress of the house. Although he claimed this was an amicable separation, the media rumor mill poured out condemnation. In response, he sent a statement of self-defense to various publications, concluding with these lines:

> I most solemnly declare, then—and this I do both in my own name and in my wife's name—that all the lately whispered rumors touching the trouble, at which I have glanced, are abominably false. And whosoever repeats one of them, after this denial, will lie as willfully and as foully as it is possible for any false witness to lie, before heaven and earth.[7]

Defending himself publicly was surely not all he did to protect his name. "When Dickens spurned his wife," writes Essie Fox, he treated her viciously, "causing Catherine the cruellest of humiliations by publishing public letters in which he claimed her to be demented, preventing her from seeing her children and even denying her the chance to attend one daughter's wedding day."[8]

This apparent hatred was evident in his relationships with other women as well. In one instance, when he had a strong disagreement with the popular writer Elizabeth Gaskell, he wrote, "If I were Mr. Gaskell O Heaven how I would beat her."[9] One wonders how much he might have beaten his wife, Catherine. Such misogyny can be seen in his writing as well. In *Oliver Twist*, Nancy is brutally murdered by Bill Sikes. When Dickens himself performed the part of Bill in a staged version, he acted "out of violence . . . with bloodthirsty relish."[10]

In *Great Expectations*, Pip discovers his sister, Mrs. Joe, "lying without sense or movement on the bare boards where she had been knocked down by a tremendous blow on the back of the head . . . destined never to be on the Rampage again."[11] Judith Johnston, in an article titled "Women and Violence in Dickens' *Great Expectations*," writes that Mrs. Joe is now portrayed as a much better woman: "Violence has rendered her a passive human being, and although her mind and hearing are irretrievably impaired, her temper is greatly improved . . . The harridan and termagant has been effectively silenced."[12]

Mrs. Joe was a harridan and a termagant, two of many words used to silence and blame women. Catherine Dickens was also regarded as the termagant, the shrew, who was responsible for the marriage breakdown.

How many words are there that refer to a belligerent—or sex-crazed—man? What about a woman? Termagant, harridan, shrew, scold, hag, battle-ax, crone, nag, hussy, bitch, slut (and dozens more, were I to scan rap lyrics). The woman is accused of henpecking and nagging her husband and getting into a catfight when she argues with another woman. Where are the comparable terms for men? The man is strong and confident and forceful, the head of the home. Female blame as much as female guilt is so much a part of our culture and worldview that we aren't even aware of it.

This is not to say that women never behave badly. They surely do. We see it in the Bible, too, in the three celebrated wives of the patriarchs—Sarah, Rebekah, and Rachel. All three of them are manipulative and treat others very poorly. But there are no scriptural terms that set them apart as "bitches" in comparison to their badly misbehaving husbands and sons.

It is true that women are often treated badly in the Bible. The "texts of terror" prove it. But so are men. How often are they slaughtered in battle or executed on the spot or swallowed up in the quicksand of a giant sinkhole? We can weep over the "texts of terror," but when we have dried our eyes, let us weep over the countless men whose suffering was no less. The Bible is a violent book, and no one is spared. Let us be grateful that the ill-behaved women don't have descriptive slurs attached to their names.

Here the issue is the nonbiblical words and actions that are regularly employed to demean women—often in the name of God or of male headship. And here the issue is domestic violence. There is no excuse *ever* for domestic violence, no matter how badly the abused one is behaving. David Duyst should have ended the marriage through a valid court procedure. Now he is spending (hopefully) the rest of his life in prison, having been forced to go through the court system himself. So it was also for Clarence Ratliff. If either one of these men believed their wives were bitches, they had many other options that did not involve murder. So it is for all of those men who beat their wives.

That was true when I was beaten on the last Mother's Day before our separation. We had argued in the afternoon about paying our church pledge. He was in control of our finances and refused to write a check for the pledge. Finally he ended the argument by telling me to "go wash the dishes" and behave like a submissive wife.

That order may have seemed like an ordinary slur, except for one important detail. He had previously forbidden me to wash dishes. He claimed I wasted too much water. He would let them pile up in the sink and would then use his own *waterless* method. I smoldered under the restriction, hating the messy, smelly sink, but he was the "head of the home from the kitchen to the bedroom." Now he, without even realizing what he was saying, was ordering me to "go do the dishes." I pivoted and marched straight to the kitchen, defiantly saying, "I will." I proceeded to run water, vowing to get the job done. He followed me, ordering me to stop. I fired back, "You told me to wash dishes, and I will." I refused to stop washing despite his demand. The next thing I knew, I was on the floor, the wind having been knocked out of me by a violent blow to my back.

Carlton was screaming. That's all I knew. When Carlton began pulling me across the floor and helping me crawl upstairs to the bedroom, he was still crying out, repeatedly asking if I was okay. I didn't know. At the moment, my legs were like rubber; I couldn't even walk. Carlton got me in bed and barred the door. He later went downstairs. I never did learn what happened between him and his father. But he later came back and was relieved to learn that I had been able to get out of bed and make it to the bathroom on my own. He said how terribly sorry he was. But then he added a statement that I'll never forget as long as I live: "Mom, it was your fault. You should have stopped doing dishes the second he said so." Here was my beloved son blaming me for having gotten beat up.

Carlton was right. The most painful part of his childhood was seeing his mother beat up, and I had done something I absolutely should not have done. I will never know why I kept washing those dishes for even five seconds after my violent ex-husband told me to stop. I had walked away so many times before or had gone into a fetal position when he knocked me to the floor. Why? Why not this time? If I hadn't cared about my own physical (and emotional) well-being, I surely should have cared for Carlton's. He was right. That he blamed me was the only way he could save himself. Blaming his father and risking a violent encounter himself would have done no good. He knew I would accept the blame. I did. Never again did I defy his father.

I carry guilt for that experience and others as well, including my indecisiveness about getting Carlton out of that house of horrors. If we had escaped earlier, would things have worked out better? Or might a judge have said Carlton was too young to testify and simply acceded to his father's demand for joint custody? I'll never know if I made the right decision in this case and in many other instances. Like many mothers, guilt is simply part of my genetic code.

But there was a period of decision making in our marriage for which I bear far greater guilt—a guilt so great it will always haunt me. (For any readers tempted to contact me with Bible verses or online therapy, please leave me alone.)

I'd like to be able to say my husband alone will have to answer one day for the terrible wrongs, but I was complicit—the queen of cover-up until the very last months of our marriage. Midway through our marriage, after he had been arrested and dismissed as minister in Woodstock, we moved to Crown Point, Indiana. Here he was able to get another small church and enroll at a seminary, which kept him away from home three days a week.

During this time, we arranged to have thirteen-year-old Deana live with us as a foster daughter. I had read books and articles on foster care and believed this was a good time in my life to help a child while she was in transition. Deana had come to our home with a few clothes in a plastic bag. When she left on June 24, 1977, more than a year later, she had stylish outfits, a bicycle, a sewing machine, a set of luggage, and several hundred dollars in a bank account. The caseworker had raved about what a great foster family we were.

She left with a lot of stuff—and also with a big secret.

A week earlier, when my ex-husband had been away at seminary for three days, I looked out the kitchen window one afternoon and noticed our older neighbor, who often paid Deana for odd jobs, patting her on the behind and behaving in an inappropriate way. I called her in, saying I had something for her to do. Actually, I was headed to the food mart a couple of blocks away across the highway, and I wanted her to stay close by, since Carlton was napping. But my main point was to tell her to never let a man treat her the way our neighbor just had.

She retorted that every man is that way. "He's no different from anyone else." I was indignant. "How can you say that? Can you even imagine Dad doing that?" There was a pause. No answer. And then she burst into tears, telling me how he had come into her room at night—more than once—and sexually abused her. Deana had lied about things before, but this was no lie. My brain shut down. I was in shock. I don't even know if I responded to her. I didn't know what I was doing. I had my money, and I headed out to purchase milk. The next thing I knew was the sound of brakes and blasting of a semitruck horn. I was crossing the highway on the way to the store.

Poor Deana! I wasn't there for her. When my ex-husband returned home, I confronted him with my knowledge of what had happened, and he finally admitted it. My rage that had been building knew no bounds. There was no physical violence, but never before or after had I felt or unleashed such virulent and deep primal wrath. Otherwise, that period in my life is little more than an awful, blurry stain of filth and regret.

She did not report him, nor did I. I was the adult; she was the kid. My reasons were not to protect my husband. My feelings of anger against him were unbounded. I did not report him because I knew he would be arrested, lose his job—our only income—and probably be imprisoned up to fifteen years. How would I manage with a two-year-old son? But mainly I didn't report him because I wanted to shield myself from the humiliation of facing family, neighbors, church members. I didn't report him for selfish reasons. I was protecting myself, and no one else.

The Bible church minister who imagined himself to be a "marriage counselor" told me I had done right in this situation—that my submission to my husband was submission to God and that I should feel no guilt. He lied to me. What I did was terribly wrong. I was complicit in this crime. I never saw Deana again.

It was Friday, June 17, 1994. I had been in Chicago for professional meetings but had left early to accomplish a mission I had been contemplating for more than a year. Carlton had by then graduated from high school, and I was beginning to get on my feet financially. I was out to fulfill a fantasy. I was going to track down Deana. Her extended family was from northern Indiana, and I had a bucket of quarters, enough to make dozens of calls from a pay phone.

I had turned on the radio to catch up on the news as I drove south on I-94, and quickly realized that the only news was the minute-by-minute account of O. J. Simpson on his mission to evade police. A *Los Angeles Times* writer summed up the story succinctly: "The O. J. Simpson 'white Bronco' chase was one of the most surreal moments in the history of Los Angeles criminal justice."[13] It truly was surreal. Here I am driving on a freeway, and the news is essentially no news because nothing is happening (apart from the gruesome fact that Simpson's wife, Nicole, had been viciously murdered) except that Simpson is in a white Bronco, which is being pursued by police officers.

Reaching northern Indiana on my way back to Grand Rapids, I exited the highway and turned off the radio. I stopped at a gas station and pulled up to a nearby phone booth with a chained northern Indiana phone book. Soon I was calling every person in the book with the last name of Judge. No luck, until finally a woman gave me a number for an individual who might know a relative who may be able to help track down this young woman.

An elderly man answered. I asked about Deana. He said he knew her and that she lived not so far away but he couldn't remember where. My heart was pounding. Is she married? Does she have a family? Is there anyone I could call who could give me more information? "Let me ask my wife." I heard what sounded like a woman's voice in the background. He kept asking, "Are you sure that was Deana?" Then I heard him say, "Yeah, you're right. It was Deana. Her sister never went to the university in Bloomington; she's the one who got married." He turned back to me and recounted the story.

Deana was a university student returning to see her sister in northern Indiana over Christmas break. Her car had slipped off a bridge in an ice storm, and the vehicle was not found until spring, at which time her body was identified.

When I hung up the phone, I was weeping so hard I could not drive. I sat in the car for more than an hour, trying to control my heaving so I could get back on the road again.

My dream had been to get Deana's phone number, call ahead, and ask her if I could stop by and see her. I knew she would say yes. She would now have been in her late twenties. Maybe she would have young children; perhaps she was a single mother. In my fantasy, I would notice that she had bags of clothes ready to be taken to the laundromat. I would go with her and the kids and renew our acquaintance. Then I would take them out to eat before heading over to Sears, where I would buy her a new washer and dryer. I would tell her how sorry I was. I would plead for her forgiveness. And I would hope to become a surrogate grandmother to her little ones.

That dream was dashed . . .

Two chapters ago, I was stomping my foot and telling my story with boldness. When my husband asked if it was hard for me to recount my story of marital rape, I quoted Lucrece: "Go get me hither paper, ink, and pen." Today, after John returned from visiting his ninety-nine-year-old mother and ninety-seven-year-old second mother-in-law, he asked how things were going. I tried to tell him what I was working on but got choked up. He said, "Oh, you're writing about Deana?" I nodded.

It's the hardest writing I have done in this book, and *getting me hither* my Apple notebook is not what is lacking. It's rather the emotional wherewithal to get the words on the screen.

I will have the opportunity to tell the rest of my story in the next chapter—among other things, my discovery of how absolutely wonderful marriage can be when there is no fear and no violence, no guilt and no blame. My marriage to John, of course, is far more than simply one without any abuse. And it has a *happily ever after* ending.

Deana's voice is silent. What if I had made a very critically different choice? What if we had gone to court together? What if I had stood by her and kept in contact with her as best I could, knowing I could not prevent social services from finding her a better home? What if . . . ? What if I had remained her advocate, never abandoning her? Is it possible she'd be alive today to tell her story with a *happily ever after* ending?

The questions haunt me.

12

vows of mutuality

Enjoying Equality in Marriage

> When entering into a marriage one
> ought to ask oneself: Do you believe
> you are going to enjoy talking with this
> person up into your old age? Everything
> else in marriage is transitory.
>
> **FRIEDRICH NIETZSCHE**

It seems impossible that I fell in love on Word of Life Island in 1967, having just graduated from college. That makes me old. Indeed, I've sometimes wondered as I have been writing these lines if my story would be more relevant if I were in my twenties or thirties? But late sixties? Do I have anything to say to young women who are dating and dreaming of marriage today? I certainly hope so. But I also hope that my message resonates with older women who have endured decades of despair in marriage.

I do not assume that most women in my situation could testify to a very satisfying second marriage. But long before John and I courted and married, I was able to say that, despite awful abuse, I did not regret my first marriage. I see how each step followed another. I would not be where I am today without that flight of fancy on Word of Life Island, without that fateful decision to marry someone who was unfit to be a husband and father.

Were those steps predetermined by God? Was the abuse predetermined? Was my marriage to John predetermined? Such philosophical brainteasers are beyond the scope of this book, but without the abuse, I would not have separated from my husband, and it necessarily follows that I would not be married to John. Where, then, would I be today? I've talked to women in this situation. Some are absolutely miserable; others alleviate their misery by finding friends outside the marriage. Husbands are bound by the Bible to love their wives. No church should ever stand by a husband who treats his wife badly, and no woman should feel trapped in such a marriage. Sometimes divorce is the only option.

"Man is condemned to be free . . . because, once thrown into the world, he is responsible for everything he does."[1] True, these are not the words of Calvin or even the Wisdom of Solomon, but Jean-Paul Sartre also has wisdom to ponder. And depending on my mood, I often make his lines my own. But then how do we deal with the burdensome responsibility of our choices?

For me to regret my falling into temptation, deceived by the serpent, in that Adirondack island garden paradise so many years ago, is almost to regret giving birth to Carlton, who is father of Kayla, and to regret marrying John and inheriting two stepdaughters and sons-in-law and three delightful grandkids. So the world turns. How do I explain this life of mine? I don't pretend to know the answers. And I often don't even know what questions to ask.

A lot of water has rolled over the dam since Carlton and I made our escape in 1987. We have both remained in Grand Rapids, sometimes seeing each other three or four times a week, other times going for weeks without even talking on the phone. The strangest aspect of my 1987 separation was my ex-husband's abandonment of Carlton.

During most of that first year, he and Carlton spent Saturdays out at Lake Michigan, but then in late summer, he moved away without leaving a forwarding address. He and Carlton saw each other once after that, and then he simply vanished.

Life was busy for Carlton and me, and Carlton insisted that his dad's abandonment was his own business. In fact, he told me his youth director had come alongside him after Christmas and asked if he had gotten a phone call from his dad. When Carlton said he had not, the youth pastor hugged him and told him how sorry he was. Carlton shrugged as he told me, saying he had tried to play along. Then he added (referring to the youth director), "He doesn't know Dad. That's just how Dad is."

But for his father not to have contact with his son for almost two decades? Had the custody arrangement been reversed I would have been almost out of my mind. And I certainly would have been taking every opportunity to be with Carlton.

The Bible is not known for stories of good marriages. In fact, if divorce were as easy to acquire in the ancient world as it is today, marriages would have been breaking up right and left among God's habitually unfaithful followers. Wives would be abandoned, no questions asked. But sons? Would a father abandon his son? Hardly. Abraham loved Ishmael and gave him up only after Sarah's rampage. David loved his disloyal son Absalom and wept uncontrollably upon hearing of his death.

The best thing a wife could ever do for a husband was to bear him a son. The biblical genealogies are critical in this ancient landscape, and they progress from father to son. Didn't Carlton's father even care about his descendants? About seeing his only son grow to manhood? About talking sports with him—the Tigers, the Lions, the Pistons, the Red Wings? Didn't he care about holding a granddaughter in his arms? Apparently not.

What is so mystifying about his abandonment of Carlton is that he for a time, apart from abusing me, was a good father. As a little family of three, we had moved in 1978, when Carlton was four, from Crown Point, Indiana, to what I had hoped would be a wonderful new life in Grand Rapids. I was somehow able to move beyond the awfulness relating to Deana, and now this was a dream come true. Both my ex-husband and I were hired to be teachers at Grand Rapids School of the Bible and Music, my position part-time. We purchased a nice home in an integrated neighborhood one long block away from the school. The campus became Carlton's second home.

I got along very well with John Miles, the school's founder and president. But our easy interaction ended after a conversation—his telling me he was very troubled by my husband. He said he was uncomfortable around him and that he found him to be very sneaky. He simply could not trust him.

Is it a sin for a wife to lie in order to protect her husband? I suppose the Bible church minister doubling as a marriage counselor would have said no, it is not a sin—that submission to a husband (and therefore to God) might require such. I lied. Not because I was submissive. I lied because I wanted so desperately for this employment situation to work out. I told Mr. Miles (as everyone called him) that I had no idea what he was referring to, that I regarded my husband to be trustworthy. Mr. Miles knew I was lying. My ex-husband was soon demoted and then terminated after he had finished his sixth year at the school. I continued teaching for two more years until I could no longer juggle my responsibilities there with my schedule at Trinity.

Some years later, I had another personal encounter with Mr. Miles after he had retired as president. He happened to be driving by one afternoon, saw me out raking, and stopped. I invited him in, and we talked. He knew my marriage had ended.

I reminded him of an incident several years earlier. I had left the campus late after my evening course, delayed by a student who needed extra help. I was walking south on Giddings when I realized a car was coming very slowly behind me, though not passing. There had been some incidents in the neighborhood. My heart was pounding. I was carrying books and a heavy briefcase, wearing a skirt and heels. I noticed lights on in neighboring houses and thought of how I might drop my books and race to a front porch for safety.

The car continued keeping pace with me, as fast as I was walking and as hard as my heart was pounding. Then I could see my own house in the distance, as I was now almost loping down the sidewalk. Suddenly, the terror was over. I heard the cranky voice of Mr. Miles. He was furious. He scolded me, reminding me that the rule for students applied also to faculty: *no walking alone after dark*. It was dangerous, and I was foolish not to have called a security guard or him or my husband to escort me. He waited in his car until I was inside the house before he drove away.

I tried to jog his memory of that night, but he had forgotten. But I didn't let the matter go. I chided him for assuming I would be safe behind locked doors. I told him I had walked that long block hundreds of times and that I had never even once been attacked in the neighborhood. It was *inside* that house, not *outside*, where I was assaulted.

He did not point out that he had tried to get me to open up. He did not point out that if I had poured my heart out to him that day in his office, he would have made sure I was safe. He did not point out that he would have gone to the mat for me in a custody battle and would have made certain my teaching salary was enough for me to support Carlton. He didn't have to. I knew that.

In the nine years we lived in Grand Rapids prior to our separation, my ex-husband was fired from three successive jobs: one teaching position and two editorial positions. How was he able to obtain these jobs? The simple answer is that he was charming, articulate, and intelligent.

This is a critical point. Someone reading this book might easily imagine I was married to a mentally disturbed man who could easily be identified as an abuser. But that was not the case. My ex-husband's only outwardly identifiable trait was his strong opposition to women in ministry and equal partnerships in marriage and the accompanying misogyny, though well disguised in public. I have no doubt there are also abusers who profess to be egalitarians. But a strong stance against women's equality should be seen as a red flag.

By 1988, Carlton and I were floundering through life. He graduated from high school with no academic honors. Among the popularity awards, however, he was voted class clown. Actually, that was no small achievement, considering that 62 percent of his large high school was made up of minority students, mainly black. His humor and easygoing manner won him many friends.

The biggest change in our relationship came when he announced at age twenty that he and Melissa were getting married. We were at O'Hare, just the two of us, on our way to Florida for a short vacation. We were on the moving walkway between concourses B and C. My heart sank. He was way too immature to be a husband—and father. Is Melissa pregnant? Amid the airport bustle, I was unable to catch his response, except that I knew it wasn't no. But by the time we had gone up the escalator and found our gate, I was tenuously ecstatic. How could I not be? This would not be another abortion statistic. This baby would be wanted, and I was going to be a grandmother. What could be more thrilling than that? And I loved Melissa.

An auto accident brought Kayla into the world two and a half months early. After spending weeks in a neonatal unit, she arrived home with a monitor. Home was my home, where I had hired a carpenter to join two bedrooms to make an upstairs suite. It was surely not the ideal, but better than living on the street. Carlton adored his darling daughter and was in many ways a great father. But he was anything but a great husband. The marriage was breaking down even before the wedding. Then months later, amid tears, I helped Melissa and tiny Kayla move out (behind Carlton's back). I bought her a microwave as a housewarming gift for her new apartment.

Should I have been surprised that the marriage ended so quickly? Not if I had read statistics. They were barely more than children themselves, and both sets of their parents were divorced. Over the years, their relationship improved. They learned to enjoy sitting together at Kayla's school functions. Together they have snapped pictures as she and her boyfriend headed out the door for the prom. And one day, they will join in giving her away in marriage and welcoming grandchildren—a lineage that will continue despite abuse, divorce, and parental abandonment.

Now in college, Kayla is a confident and resolute student, balancing her classes, her job as a bistro server, her editing at the school newspaper, and a serious boyfriend. Life is good. And life is very good for me since 2004 when I married John. His marital background couldn't be more different from mine. In marrying him, I knew this was not a union between the two of us alone. I was joining him and the abiding memories of two dearly departed wives. Our marriage ceremony included singing a rewrite of "Will the Circle Be Unbroken," and a remembrance by name of those who had gone on before us—my parents, his father, and especially his beloved first and second wives.

John first married his high school sweetheart (she, too, named Ruth Ann). A picture of her and John sits on a shelf near my desk. I look across and see it even now as I'm writing. She was a nurse with an earthy sense of humor. For a time she worked in the hospital emergency room, always poised for the worst. She was good, and she knew it. If there was going to be a terrible accident, she wanted to be right there as the gurney came through the door. She was capable of quickly assessing a situation and giving orders. She saw things a doctor might have missed. She saved lives—all but her own.

It was a dark day when she and John were given the diagnosis of stage 3 ovarian cancer. The odds were not good. Surgeries, chemotherapies, alternative medicines followed, even as she carried on for three years with work, church activities, vacations, and fussing over a grandson and then a granddaughter. She knew the medical community, and she had the best care possible, but she succumbed to cancer shortly after daughter Laura's summer wedding to Bob. Near the end, she was so thin that it's hard to look at her picture packed away with other family photos. I have come to know her through John, through her dear daughters, and through her beautiful, smiling face in the picture as she cuddles close to her beloved husband. They were faithful to each other for thirty-seven years, till death did them part.

Little more than a year later, John had a new bride. He had known her from a distance at Calvin College and at church. Then he heard she had been diagnosed with pancreatic cancer. He sought her out just to give her encouragement, only to realize she was the one who was encouraging him, having known of his loss. Soon there was a get-together for coffee, then for dinner—and within months they were inseparable. But when John mentioned marriage, Myra held back. Never before married, she was independent and was not about to entangle someone else in her deadly serious medical issues. She was talked down by a persistent lover, and with the support of all her delighted friends, she took the plunge. They married in early October and honeymooned at Thistledowne at Seul Choix, a lovely remote bed-and-breakfast on the northern shore of Lake Michigan.

Soon after that, I became acquainted with Myra. We were connected by a mutual friend who knew we were both struggling with difficult work-related situations. We often got together and commiserated, understanding so well what the other was going through. But more than that, we had lively conversations about every issue imaginable.

Before earning a PhD in education (with a specialty in learning disabilities) at Northwestern University, Myra had been an elementary schoolteacher. As a professor at Calvin, she stepped out of the insular atmosphere and developed strong collegial relationships with professors at nearby universities. She was a sponge, soaking in and experimenting with their research findings, a pattern that wasn't always appreciated by colleagues. She interacted easily on almost any subject—except for her terminal illness. I asked her about this on occasion. Always appearing optimistic, she would brush off concerns and optimistically explain a new chemotherapy.

I'll never forget the midnight Christmas Eve service as I was walking amid the crowd in the center aisle. She was ahead of me and managed to get my attention. She suggested we sit on a bench. She'd had a long day. She talked mostly about the three grandchildren and how much fun it was to open presents. She laughed and talked as though she didn't have a care in the world. We parted as cheerfully as we began.

The next day, I packed for a flight to Phoenix, meeting my sister for hiking in Tucson and Sedona. I had no cell phone in those days, and I left my computer at home. On my return, when I retrieved emails, the messages were all the same: Myra had died. Impossible. I had just talked with her. She was doing so well. I later learned from John that what she didn't tell me was that they had met with someone from hospice on the morning of Christmas Eve. Typical Myra. She wanted no pity, and the last thing she would think of doing was to spoil a jolly conversation with news that she had only a few days left to live.

Through John, I have come to know Myra even better. Before she and John married, Mom (Myra's mother) tells how she had expressed her fears to Dad, wondering how her independent daughter would be able to manage being married. Dad simply grinned and said, "I think John can handle her." As it turned out, at least from my outsider's perspective, "*she* handled him."

John tells stories about his "handling" her. She was an art collector, to the extent a professor living on a modest income can afford to be. She had purchased a large, striking original painting and had taken it to be framed. When she and John arrived to pick it up, she scrutinized the finished product, carefully examining it up close and from a distance. Then she said, "That won't work." John and the framer were stunned. The framer pointed out that she had carefully chosen the frame and that he could not return her payment. From the studio John and Myra moved to the parking lot as tempers flared. It ended with John pacing the parking lot and Myra ordering a new frame.

On another occasion, they had hired the services of a professional to paint Myra's office in their condo. Once the work was completed, Myra realized that now the walls and furniture were at odds. The room needed a somewhat different hue. John was furious. She insisted there was no alternative, and she would do the repainting. Recognizing her superior sense of feng shui, John insisted on doing it himself, a task he actually enjoyed, though not without rubbing it in. With each telling of those stories, I love Myra more. Sure, she was a perfectionist. But she was so much more than that. She had a flare for fun, for throwing parties, inviting her friends for good food and filling the room with her lively presence.

John always says she had real class. She did, though he's quick to point out that I do too—adding that the only difference is that mine is quite low. Low class or not, I have also managed to "handle" him.

John and I had a small backyard wedding at my house on Giddings. At the crack of dawn that day, storm clouds poured down buckets of rain, soaking the basement carpet. So there I was—a water vacuum dumping gallons of water into the washtub. But the rain stopped in time for the late Saturday morning wedding, and the sun came out. John had helped prepare the house to make it perfect for our big day. We had moved a sofa to our covered deck in the back. I had raced out in the morning to cover it with a tarp. Guests came and left before we noticed that an old, torn, paint-spotted tarp was still on the sofa. I was horrified; John was in stitches.

There were other little glitches. Just before the ceremony was to begin, I noticed I had forgotten to purchase cocktail sauce for the shrimp. (I catered my own wedding, a practice I do not recommend.) Carlton was on it. He offered to drive down the street two blocks to the Miti-Mini Superette. Not trusting him, my last words hurled from my bedroom window were, "Don't you dare go any further than Miti-Mini." Long story short, that little neighborhood grocery store didn't have any, nor did another little grocery store, so he stood in line at the supermarket for cocktail sauce—while his mother, the bride, paced the upstairs floor and fumed.

Cocktail sauce delayed the wedding for forty minutes. But the sun was out. Carlton, forgiven and looking strikingly handsome, walked me onto the back deck and down the steps to where John was seated in a white Adirondack chair. One problem. He appeared to be in shock, entirely inert. He has since claimed he was so awestruck by my hat that he forgot to get up. I had to motion for him to stand. Poor henpecked groom could not even say his vows before his bride started telling him what to do. We laughed ourselves silly over those little upsets. Had the day gone perfectly, we wouldn't have stories to tell. That is how our married life began, and that is the way it has been all these years since.

(That black and white, large brimmed hat is a story unto itself. It holds secrets. I reveal only that it was very lovely, and it alone cost more than all the rest of my wedding garments put together.)

John is the least demanding man I've ever encountered. I often comment to people that he's the perfect husband, having had three strong wives to whip him into shape. He is easy to please and rarely complains. In fact, he's probably best summed up in Jerry Seinfeld's quip: "Men want the same thing from their underwear that they want from women: a little bit of support, and a little bit of freedom."

If John and I were to list all our commonalities and compatibilities, it would require, I am sure, a full ream of paper. Before we married we knew we both loved the outdoors. Biking, hiking, and kayaking were activities we could hardly live without. I added picnicking to that. He had enjoyed going out to eat with his late wives. For me, perhaps on rare occasions. But in good weather, my style is to pack something from home or purchase takeout. Even our anniversary dinner is a picnic. We shop together at Russo's deli counter and head for our favorite spot along the Grand River. Unlike any other picnic, this one comes complete with a white linen tablecloth and stemmed glassware. People have actually stopped and asked us what's going on, and then they happily congratulate us.

John hates airports with a passion, so we do our traveling by car. Every January, we drive to Big Bend National Park, where we stay at the Chisos Mountains Lodge and spend a week hiking. John had been there with Ruth and Myra, and he went there to mourn and meditate after their deaths. There is no place we love more than that incredible expanse of land bordered by the Rio Grande River.

Every fall, we make a pilgrimage to Spooner in northern Wisconsin to the farm and the nearby town where I grew up. While there, we drive around to my old haunts, John enjoying it as much as I do. We visit the run-down one-room school were I spent first grade, seated not far from my older brother and sister. To celebrate our sixty-fifth and seventieth birthdays, we kayaked the Yellow River for three days, biking back to spend each night in Spooner. Our paddling took us by familiar homes of cousins and neighbors and right through the farm on which I grew up, now owned by my younger brother.

In addition to travel and outdoor activities, another pastime that binds us tightly together is John's reading to me every morning and every night. He sits up in the bed as I lie beside him. We both love history and Southern or British fiction, not to mention the edgy books we've read together on biblical or theological themes. Our favorite magazine is *The New Yorker*, and I'll often hand him a section to read aloud to me. We love to experience good writing or a good cartoon together. And it seems as though almost every day, after I have glanced over some particularly good essay on the Internet, I'll ask him to sit at the screen and read it aloud.

Soon after we married, John and I made two life-defining critical decisions (and many lesser ones). The first was to purchase a low-priced home in a flood plain on the Grand River, several miles north of Grand Rapids. Together we transformed it with the help of a competent carpenter. We love living in that river-rat community. No one puts on airs. And we are all bound together by floods. On any given season, we can expect at least a fourteen-foot flood, which means our house sits on an island, and we kayak in and out to higher ground where we park our car. In April 2013, we went through the hundred-year flood, with the river actually in our house.

Perhaps the most significant decision we made was to carry on with a little garden-and-gift business we now operate together. In the late 1990s, when my teaching at Trinity was winding down, I opened a business with Carlton, whose academic life was faltering. Soon Carlton Gardens was up and running. Shortly after that, however, I was contacted by Calvin Seminary, and my teaching career resumed. Carlton moved on to bigger and better things, and the business floundered.

After John and I married, however, through the encouragement of friends, we decided to bring the business back to life. John, having retired early (as professor of music at Calvin College) during Ruth's final months of illness, was eager to take up carpentry, a trade that was the occupation of his grandfather and a dream of his father. So on this wonderful little acre of land (with an original house and garage transformed into the main showrooms), he has built outbuildings, including a charming little chapel complete with a plaque in memory of Ruth Ann and Myra Jean.

Now John and I work together every day. He is involved in carpentry projects, while I'm writing, painting, and waiting on customers who wander in. I had never imagined I could be with a person virtually 24/7 and still get along so well, though admittedly the business is spacious enough to keep us out of each other's hair.

Since reading *Love and War* by Mary Matalin and James Carville, I've reflected a great deal on how they have maintained their love for each other amid such significant differences, and not only in matters of politics. Their very personalities seem to be entirely at odds. I've asked myself, ever since I began following them in the 1992 political campaigns, if I could survive in a marriage like that.

Like them, John and I have strong opinions on many things. But we share the same worldview. Unlike the Matalin-Carville marriage, ours is not centered on fighting those battles. After finding my own voice during seventeen years of singleness, it would have been hard to settle into a marriage to someone whose social, political, and religious views were significantly at odds with my own.

On little matters of household roles, many things have just fallen into place. He putters around the kitchen and concocts interesting meals. He also runs the dishwasher. I take care of the laundry. We shovel snow, rake, and generally enjoy gardening together. In fact, it might sound like John and I have a marriage made in heaven. Well, not quite. We have our differences. In fact, sometimes it seems like we're bickering about things that are utterly inconsequential.

John is a walking encyclopedia and dictionary combined. We're right now driving through southern Mississippi, and the road sign pointed to the town of Lux. He can't help himself. He not only defines the Latin word, but then the phrase *lux perpetua* (perpetual light). "Let *lux perpetua* shine upon them"—part of the Latin Mass. He can even quote love songs in Latin. But at the same time, he struggles with saying those three little words that are so essential for a meaningful relationship. Maybe it's harder for men than women, but through my loving encouragement—and perhaps a little sarcasm—he's now able at appropriate times to say those rare words: *I don't know.*

An almost everyday topic that we bicker about relates to words. I'm the writer in the family; he edits and cannot go through an afternoon without his crosswords. Words are everything to us. He brought the massive two-volume *OED* (*Oxford English Dictionary*) into our marriage, and he somehow manages to make it work for him most of the time. Tonight we were nattering about the word *toilet*. I defined it as "a commode" or "an outhouse," like the one-holer I used as a kid when I went to the *toilet*. He grabbed volume 2 to prove me wrong. From *toilet* he turned to *commode*. I don't think the *OED* wordsmiths are correct, but John is still crowing about his verbal skills.

Another daily matter. John strongly objects to my coaching him while he drives, and he even objects to my term *coaching*. All three of us wives have had no doubt that we are better drivers than he is. In fact, his first wife, Ruth, forced him into the passenger seat when roads got slippery. Myra and I, both having driven tractors since we were six, simply came by driving intuitively. I risk his displeasure by saying this, but he drives *like a woman*.

I have my own Mother Goose lines that mimic the familiar rhyme: "Jack Sprat could eat no fat, his wife could eat no lean, and so betwixt them both, they lick'd the platter clean." Right there, we see in the Sprats a serious marital difference, but they solve it amicably. Our situation, too, might someday be solved:

John Worst did not drive fast,
his wife could not slow down,
and so betwixt them both,
they walked about the town.

Our most heated arguments have related to his recycling. I'm a saver; he recycles. "When are you going to throw away these papers," he growls. So I sort papers. All well and good, until he recycles that critical article or the receipt needed for tax purposes. There is, I'm convinced, such a thing as recycling sin. In fact, on one occasion, both of us searched high and low for hours and failed to find a musical score he had finished the day before. On the ruse of picking up a grocery item, he drove to the recycling center. Finding it closed, he crawled on his stomach under the metal fence and went through the bin where he suspected he had dumped it. The good news: he wasn't arrested; the bad news: he didn't find it. After he returned home and confessed his sin, I ordered penance. I told him to go up to his study where he had done the work and to meditate for as long as it took to remember where he had put it. In less than a half hour, his deep thoughts took him to the file cabinet and to our 2013 tax documents that he had worked on the previous day.

Ours is a marriage of mutuality. But I ordered him to do penance. Was I, then, assuming the *headship* in our marriage? Sure. And John sometimes assumes headship. I am the boss every Christmas when a complimentary box of chocolates arrives in the mail addressed to me. I open it and offer one to him and then pick one for myself. Then I hide the box, and they last for the next ten days. He simply can't be trusted as boss of the chocolates. Together we savor chocolates. More than that, we savor marriage.

For John and me, the game of baseball offers a metaphor for marriage. He's had three home runs. I struck out and went back to the dugout, my head hanging low. But the next time at bat, I hit a homer out of the park.

I close with the striking words of Arista in Michael Sullivan's novel *Heir of Novron*:

> *How can you regret never having found true love?*
> *That's like saying you regret not being born a genius.*
> *People don't have control over such things.*
> *It either happens or it doesn't.*
> *It's a gift—a present that most never get.*
> *It's more like a miracle, really, when you think of it.*
> *I mean, first you have to find that person,*
> *and then you have to get to know*
> *them to realize just what*
> *they mean to you—that right there*
> *is ridiculously difficult.*
> *Then . . . that person has to feel the same way about you.*
> *It's like searching for a specific snowflake,*
> *and even if you manage to find it, that's not good enough.*
> *You still have to find its matching pair.*
> *What are the odds?*[22]

afterword

Tackling the Tough Questions

The unexamined life is not worth living.

SOCRATES

Perhaps Socrates overstates his case, but it is important for us to examine our lives. Indeed, one of the reasons I so appreciate the apostle Paul is that he examines his life—often through storytelling. I'm a storyteller. In fact, all of my writing in one way or another is an exercise in storytelling. I take the Bible as my model. It's a book filled with honest, eye-opening, and often heart-wrenching stories propelled by rivers of heartache, anger, embarrassment, uncertainty, temptation, regret. In them we see our own sins and struggles reflected on the water. These narratives beg for explication and application.

Yes, I am a storyteller. But never before have I told my own story. Never before have I examined and put into writing a significant and secretive aspect of my life. As with stories in the Bible, I urge readers to think deeply about these dysfunctional decades I endured and also the years of struggle and happiness that followed. But these stories are surely not mine alone. Whether they belong to Elizabeth Packard,

Judge Carol Irons, Meredith Viera, or Mary Winkler, the narratives have profound implications.

Alongside the stories, I have woven the two-sided conversation in Christian circles today relating to marriage—headship versus equality. Actually, it's often less a conversation than a heated argument—one that sometimes degenerates into angry wrangling.

Millions of Christians in North America and millions more around the world have ties with churches or parachurch ministries that strongly affirm male headship in marriage. Here women (and men) are often barraged with mixed messages. The concepts of headship and submission are often assumed to be cut-and-dried. But are they? Is a wife, for example, "graciously submitting" (to use Southern Baptist terminology) if she is standing up for herself and challenging her husband's authority on matters that may involve physical and emotional abuse? There would be no need for her to make the challenge, headship proponents argue, if the husband is fulfilling his role. After all, the complete phrase reads, "A wife is to submit herself graciously to the servant leadership of her husband"—which is comparable to the "headship of Christ."

Again I bring to mind Socrates, in this case to employ what is called the Socratic method—to understand a subject by asking questions.

If the husband is the head—the ruler—in the home, who regulates him? Who determines if his headship is actually comparable to the headship of Christ? The husband himself? Is he alone the interpreter of the biblical standard? Is he the judge and jury in his own court case? Is he the referee, the umpire, in his own ball game? Is he absolutely unbiased? Who determines exactly what male headship entails in each situation? Is there a written or unwritten standard for twenty-first-century domestic situations? At what point, if ever, does his behavior make his headship invalid? Indeed, what are the consequences when husbands fail to live up to this standard?

Does this standard apply only to a husband? Indeed, when does male headship begin? How do boys and single men prepare to rule a wife? Is headship training available? Do they practice in high school?

How should boys and men respond to female "headship" of teachers, corporate managers, a police officer, a wife who is a police chief?

And what about submission? How do girls and young women prepare for submitting to their husbands? Do teenage girls have full equality with their male counterparts? Do they have full equality when courting? During the engagement period? Does their submission begin only at the moment they say "I do"? What prepares a bride for such a drastic change if she is a corporate manager with an MBA, her supervisor a woman who emphasizes teamwork and collaboration over power and authority?

How does male headship play out on a practical level in marriage? When serious differences arise in marriage, how is the husband's rule enforced? Does his headship allow him to physically prevent his wife from making phone calls, from leaving the house, from using a vehicle? Does his headship give him sole control over money and permit him to deny his wife access to financial records? Does it allow him to confiscate a manuscript or to make a major decision without her consent? Does it ever involve corporal punishment?

And what does a wife's submission entail? Does a wife's mandate to graciously submit stifle her better judgment in such things as voting or volunteering her time? Does it silence her voice in public discussions? Does it suppress the empowerment she may need to challenge her husband on immoral or unethical behavior and to demand changes? Does it curb her instinct to report him to law enforcement? Must she remain submissive to a violent husband? One who is mentally unstable? One who is impeded by dementia?

These are not simply hypothetical questions. Many of them relate to my former marriage and to women discussed in this volume. It's a disgrace to simply pass responsibility on to male church elders or to argue that egalitarian marriages are also troubled by abuse. In such marriages, the submission mandate would never be an added cross for a wife to bear. Neither partner during courtship or engagement or marriage is a ruler of the relationship or of the other individual. Each one is confronted by high biblical standards such as these:

Jesus: "So in everything, do to others what you would have them do to you." (Matthew 7:12)

Paul: "Submit to one another out of reverence for Christ." (Ephesians 5:21)

Jesus: "Love one another. As I have loved you, so you must love one another." (John 13:34)

The burden of responding to these matters lies with those who preach male headship. Here I have asked some of the dozens of critical unanswered questions that relate directly to women's stories of abuse. Sadly, there is little evidence that proponents of male headship are seriously grappling with them and speaking out publicly, and most women in such marriages are not being correctly counseled on matters of domestic violence. It is critical that there is a process in place to support such wives.

It is my sincere hope that this volume and these stories will help spark conversation and will challenge Christian leaders and laypeople on both sides of the headship debate to deal directly and biblically with the often silent epidemic of domestic abuse.

I close by reflecting on another saying often attributed to Socrates, this one related to marriage. Though humorous and sexist at the same time, it is useful nevertheless: "By all means, marry. If you get a good wife, you'll become happy; if you get a bad one, you'll become a philosopher." Considering the era in which he lived, it is significant that Socrates did not conclude with a different last line: "You'll become a wife beater."

For headship proponents, I rewrite the saying:

By all means, marry.
If you get a submissive wife,
you'll become happy;
if you get an egalitarian one,
you'll become a philosopher—a wise one.

acknowledgments

Authors are asked to promote not only their books but themselves, with book tours, book trailers, interviews, blogs, and an active social media presence. And connected to these campaigns is the most irritating promotional addendum of all: the acknowledgments page.

SAM SACKS, "AGAINST ACKNOWLEDGMENTS," *NEW YORKER*

In lieu of listing esteemed colleagues and famous friends (including Oprah and three Supreme Court justices) who offered invaluable insights as they pored over this book, I wish to thank a small team at Zondervan whose hard work and critique have added immeasurably to the final product. I am deeply indebted to Katya Covrett, executive editor, who kept very close tabs on the book from beginning to end. Twice she steered the manuscript out of a messy morass, helping me to become grounded and to see the way forward. My frequent interaction with Dirk Buursma, senior editor-at-large, in the final editing process has truly been a pleasure. Jesse Hillman, senior marketing director, has had a keen eye for detail and a commitment to carry my story to a wide audience. I would be remiss if I did not acknowledge Stanley N. Gundry, senior vice president and publisher. Without his confidence in me decades ago in the early 1980s—and since—I would not be a writer today.

Even with the best team of professionals, however, I could not have written this book without the encouragement and repeated editing of my husband, John Worst. Fully aware of the emotional toll the writing was taking, he maintained a steady hand every step of the way. He loves words, and his replacement verbs or nouns can be found, I'm sure, on every page.

notes

INTRODUCTION

1. Quoted in Danni Moss, "Paige Patterson's Views on Domestic Violence," https://dannimoss.wordpress.com/clergy-abuse-links/abuse-in-the-church/paige-pattersons-views-on-domestic-violence/ (accessed August 10, 2015).

CHAPTER 1: MOVING BEYOND HEADSHIP DEBATES

1. John Piper, quoted in "What the Bible Says about Gender Roles: A Debate," *Discernment* 4, no. 1 (Winter 1996), www.wheaton.edu/~/media/Files/Centers-and-Institutes/CACE/discernment/FamilyValues.pdf (accessed August 10, 2015).
2. Joseph Benson, *The Life of the Rev. John W. de la Flechere* (London: Thomas Cordeux, 1817), 289.
3. Robertson McQuilkin, "Muriel's Blessing," *Christianity Today*, February 5, 1996, www.christianitytoday.com/ct/1996/february5/6t2032.html (accessed August 11, 2015).
4. Ibid.
5. Ibid.
6. Ibid.
7. Ibid.
8. Cited in Dave Boehi, "Till Death Do Us Part," *Family Life*, www.familylife.com/articles/topics/marriage/staying-married/commitment/till-death-do-us-part (accessed August 11, 2015).
9. Quoted in Catherine Failoni, "An Unconditional Love," https://cfailoni.wordpress.com/non-fiction-story/ (accessed August 11, 2015).

CHAPTER 2: POLLUTION IN PARADISE

1. Word of Life Youth and Family Camps, website description, http://camps.wol.org/island/ (accessed August 11, 2015).
2. Kathryn Joyce, "Biblical Battered Wife Syndrome: Christian Women and Domestic Violence," June 18, 2009, http://religiondispatches.org/biblical-battered-wife-syndrome-christian-women-and-domestic-violence/ (accessed August 11, 2015).
3. Cited in Justin S. Holcomb and Lindsey A. Holcomb, *Is It My Fault? Hope and Healing for Those Suffering Domestic Violence* (Chicago: Moody, 2014), 22.
4. Bryce Laliberte, "Eve, the Original Feminist," August 28, 2013, anarchopapist.wordpress.com (no longer on the web).
5. Raymond C. Ortlund Jr., "Male-Female Equality and Male Headship," in *Recovering Biblical Manhood and Womanhood: A Response to Evangelical Feminism*, ed. John Piper and Wayne Grudem (Wheaton, IL: Crossway, 2006), 107.
6. Walter M. Miller Jr., *A Canticle for Leibowitz* (1959; repr., New York: HarperCollins, 2006), 242.

CHAPTER 3: MUTUALITY IN LIVING COLOR

1. Ruth A. Tucker, *Women in the Maze* (Carol Stream, IL: InterVarsity, 1992), 133.
2. Quoted in Bob Allen, "Panel Urges 'Complementarians' to Practice What They Preach," April 24, 2012, http://baptistnews.com/ministry/congregations/item/7156-panel-urges-complementarians-to-practice-what-they-preach (accessed August 11, 2015).
3. John Piper, "The Beautiful Faith of Fearless Submission," April 15, 2007, www.desiringgod.org/sermons/the-beautiful-faith-of-fearless-submission (accessed August 11, 2015).
4. John Piper, "A Vision of Biblical Complementarity," in *Recovering Biblical Manhood and Womanhood: A Response to Evangelical Feminism*, 2nd ed., ed. John Piper and Wayne Grudem (Wheaton, IL: Crossway, 2006), 52.

5. Cited in Kathryn Joyce, "'Biblical Manhood' Conference Espouses Male Supremacy," July 3, 2008, http://religiondispatches.org/biblical-manhood-conference-espouses-male-supremacy/ (accessed August 11, 2015).
6. John Chrysostom, *Homily: "The Kind of Women Who Ought to be Taken as Wives," Patrologia Graeca* 51.230.
7. Ibid.
8. Ruth A. Tucker, *Private Lives of Pastors' Wives* (Grand Rapids: Zondervan, 1988), 153–54.
9. Gustav Niebuhr, "Southern Baptists Declare Wife Should 'Submit' to Her Husband," *New York Times*, June 10, 1998, www.nytimes.com/1998/06/10/us/southern-baptists-declare-wife-should-submit-to-her-husband.html (accessed August 11, 2015).
10. Quoted in Irwin T. Hyatt Jr., *Our Ordered Lives Confess: Three Nineteenth-Century Missionaries in East Shantung* (Cambridge, MA: Harvard University Press, 1976), 104–5.
11. Cited in Patricia Gundry, *Heirs Together: Applying the Biblical Principle of Mutual Submission in Your Marriage* (Grand Rapids: Suitcase Books, 1999), 168.

CHAPTER 4: ABUSE OF POWER

1. Ruth A. Tucker, *Dynamic Women of the Bible: What We Can Learn from Their Surprising Stories* (Grand Rapids: Baker, 2014), 29.
2. Carolyn Custis James, *The Gospel of Ruth: Loving God Enough to Break the Rules* (Grand Rapids: Zondervan, 2008), 30.
3. Quoted in John W. Miller, "The Problem of Men, Reconsidered," in *Does Christianity Teach Male Headship?* ed. David Blankenhorn, Don S. Browning, and Mary Stewart Van Leeuwen (Grand Rapids: Eerdmans, 2004), 65.
4. Ibid., 66.
5. Kathryn Joyce, "Inside the Duggar Family's Conservative Ideology," *Newsweek*, March 16, 2009, www.newsweek.com/inside-duggar-familys-conservative-ideology-76547 (accessed August 11, 2015).

6. Greg Gibson, "5 Reasons Why Getting Married Young Is Still a Good Thing," http://cbmw.org/men/manhood/5-reasons-why-getting-married-young-is-still-a-good-thing/ (accessed August 11, 2015).

7. "Tim Fall Critiques Owen Strachan's 'New' Dateship: Second Verse, Same as the First," September 22, 2014, http://thewartburgwatch.com/2014/09/22/tim-fall-critiques-owen-strachans-new-dateship-second-verse-same-as-the-first/ (accessed August 11, 2015).

8. See Libby Anne, "Child Marriage and the Rest of the Maranatha Story," December 2, 2013, www.patheos.com/blogs/lovejoyfeminism/2013/12/the-rest-of-the-maranatha-story.html (accessed August 11, 2015).

9. Quoted in Julie Anne, "Christian Domestic Discipline (Wife Spanking): A Personal Story, and a Closer Look at Patterns Connected with This Abusive Practice," October 5, 2014, http://spiritualsoundingboard.com/2014/10/05/christian-domestic-discipline-wife-spanking-a-personal-story-and-a-closer-look-at-patterns-connected-with-this-abusive-practice/ (accessed August 11, 2015).

10. Russell D. Moore, "After Patriarchy, What? Why Egalitarians Are Winning the Gender Debate," *Journal of the Evangelical Theological Society* 49, no. 3 (September 2006): 573–74, emphasis in original, www.etsjets.org/files/JETS-PDFs/49/49-3/JETS_49-3_569-576_Moore.pdf (accessed August 11, 2015).

11. Carolyn Osiek, "Did Early Christians Teach, or Merely Assume, Male Headship?" in *Does Christianity Teach Male Headship?* ed. David Blankenhorn et al. (Grand Rapids: Eerdmans, 2004), 27.

CHAPTER 5: WHAT IF WOMEN RULED THE WORLD?

1. "Germaine Greer," *Wikipedia*, http://en.wikipedia.org/wiki/Germaine_Greer (accessed September 22, 2015).

2. Carolyn Gregoire, "How Men and Women Process Emotions Differently," *The Huffington Post*, January 25, 2015, http://www

.huffingtonpost.com/2015/01/25/how-men-and-women-process_n_
6510160.html (accessed August 11, 2015).

3. David M. Scholer, "Dealing with Abuse," http://
godswordtowomen.org/scholer.htm (accessed August 11, 2015).

4. Ibid.

5. "Junia," *Wikipedia*, http://en.wikipedia.org/wiki/Junia.

6. Stephen Lamb, "Some Thoughts on *Bobbed Hair, Bossy Wives,
and Women Preachers*," February 7, 2012, www.jslweb.com/
blog/2012/02/07/some-thoughts-on-bobbed-hair-bossy-wives-and-
women-preachers/ (accessed August 11, 2015).

7. Quoted in ibid.

8. Cited in Rachel Held Evans, "Inside Mark Driscoll's Disturbed
Mind," July 29, 2014, http://rachelheldevans.com/blog/driscoll-
troubled-mind-william-wallace (accessed August 11, 2015).

9. Abigail James, "'We Men Are Too Machista': Pope Francis Urges
Men to Listen to Women's Ideas More," *Catholic Online*, January
19, 2015, www.catholic.org/news/hf/faith/story.php?id=58459
(accessed August 11, 2015).

CHAPTER 6: WAS JOHN CALVIN A FEMINIST?

1. The account of John Calvin and Renée of Ferrara is drawn from
Roland H. Bainton, *Women of the Reformation: In Germany and Italy*
(Minneapolis: Augsburg, 1971).

2. Cited in Ruth A. Tucker, "John Calvin and the Princess," *Christian
History*, September 3, 2009, www.christianitytoday.com/ch/
bytopic/women/johncalvinandtheprincess.html (accessed August
11, 2015).

3. David Van Biema, "The New Calvinism," *Time*, March 12,
2009, http://content.time.com/time/specials/packages/arti
cle/0,28804,1884779_1884782_1884760,00.html (accessed August
11, 2015).

4. Austin Fischer, "Dear John Piper," *Purple Theology*, March 7, 2014,
http://purpletheology.com/dear-john-piper/ (accessed August 11,
2015).

5. See description on the website at www.desiringgod.org/books/ john-calvin-and-his-passion-for-the-majesty-of-god (accessed August 11, 2015).

6. "Letter from Calvin to an Unknown Woman," June 4, 1559, *Calvini Opera*, XVII, col. 539, in *The Register of the Company of Pastors of Geneva in the Time of Calvin*, ed. P. E. Hughes (Grand Rapids: Eerdmans, 1966), 344–45.

7. Cited in Thea B. Van Halsema, *This Was John Calvin* (Grand Rapids: Baker, 1981), 113.

8. James McClendon, *Biography as Theology: How Life Stories Can Remake Today's Theology* (Nashville: Abingdon, 1974), 14.

9. Philip C. Holtrop, *The Bolsec Controversy* (Lewiston, NY: Mellen, 1993), 669.

10. John Calvin, *Commentary on the Epistles of Paul to the Corinthians*, vol. 1 (Grand Rapids: Baker, 2003), 357–58.

11. Cited in Tucker, "John Calvin and the Princess."

12. Ibid.

13. Ibid.

14. Mary Stewart Van Leeuwen, "Whose Hospitality? Whose Kingdom?" Stob Lectureship at Calvin College and Seminary, November 4, 2003, http://bluechristian.blogspot.com/2007/10/ whose-hospitality-whose-kingdom-womens.html (accessed August 11, 2015).

15. Abstract of Ann W. Annis and Rodger R. Rice, "A Survey of Abuse Prevalence in the Christian Reformed Church," *Journal of Religion & Abuse* 3 (June 2002): 7–40, www.freepaperdownload. us/1745/Article1487484.htm (accessed August 11, 2015).

16. Ronald H. Fritze, "Married with Children: Wittenberg Style," *Age of the Reformation*, February 8, 2010, www.corndancer.com/fritze/ reformation/refmaton_arch/refmaton_katie.html (accessed August 11, 2015).

17. Susan C. Karant-Nunn and Merry E. Wiesner-Hanks, *Luther on Women: A Sourcebook* (New York: Cambridge University Press, 2003), 13.

18. Cited in Roland Bainton, *Here I Stand: A Life of Martin Luther* (1950; repr., Nashville: Abingdon, 1990), 299.

CHAPTER 7: THE RULE OF THUMB

1. Nicole Flatow, "South Carolina Prosecutors Say Stand Your Ground Doesn't Apply to Victims of Domestic Violence," October 14, 2014, http://thinkprogress.org/justice/2014/10/14/3579407/ south-carolina-prosecutors-say-stand-your-ground-doesnt-apply-to-victims-of-domestic-violence/ (accessed August 11, 2015).
2. Jone Johnson Lewis, "Rule of Thumb and Wife-Beating— Mostly a Myth," http://womenshistory.about.com/od/ mythsofwomenshistory/a/rule_of_thumb.htm (accessed August 11, 2015).
3. Reva B. Siegel, "'The Rule of Love': Wife Beating as Prerogative and Privacy," *Yale Law School Faculty Scholarship Series* (January 1, 1996): 2119, http://digitalcommons.law.yale.edu/cgi/viewcontent. cgi?article=2092&context=fss_papers (accessed August 11, 2015).
4. Ibid., 2118.
5. Ibid.
6. Barbara Sapinsley, *The Private War of Mrs. Packard: The Dramatic Story of a Nineteenth-Century Feminist* (New York: Kodansha, 1995), 66, emphasis added.
7. Ibid., 69.
8. Ibid., 71.
9. Ibid., 79.
10. Katharine Bushnell, "*Oikodespotēs*," *God's Word to Women*, https:// godswordtowomen.wordpress.com/tag/oikodespotes/ (accessed August 11, 2015).
11. Sapinsley, 7.
12. Quoted in ibid.
13. Ruth A. Tucker, *Leadership Reconsidered: Becoming a Person of Influence* (Grand Rapids: Baker, 2008), 168.
14. Cited in Michigan Officer Involved Domestic Violence Project, http://michiganoidv.blogspot.com/1994/08/officer-clarence-ratliff-grand-rapids.html (accessed August 11, 2015).

15. Cited in Bob Allen, "Southern Baptist Pastor Charged with Domestic Violence," November 20, 2007, www.ethicsdaily.com/southern-baptist-pastor-charged-with-domestic-violence-cms-11914 (accessed August 11, 2015).
16. Quoted in "Mary Winkler," *Wikipedia*, https://en.wikipedia.org/wiki/Mary_Winkler#cite_note-4 (accessed August 11, 2015).
17. Ibid.
18. Ellen Goodman, "No Acceptable Excuse for Murder," *Chicago Tribune*, May 28, 1989, http://articles.chicagotribune.com/1989-05-28/features/8902040956_1_first-female-judge-role-models-police-officer (accessed August 11, 2015).
19. "Officer Clarence Ratliff—Grand Rapids PD," Sunday, March 16, 1975, http://michiganoidv.blogspot.com/1975/03/officer-clarence-ratliff-grand-rapids.html (accessed August 11, 2015).
20. Goodman, "No Acceptable Excuse."

CHAPTER 8: STANDING AGAINST CULTURAL MISOGYNY

1. Dean Flemming, *Contextualization in the New Testament: Patterns for Theology and Mission* (Downers Grove, IL: InterVarsity, 2005), 135.
2. Cited in Joel Stephen Williams, "A Study of Galatians 3:28: The Role of Men and Women in the Church and the Home," http://www.afn.org/~afn52344/longer1.html (accessed August 11, 2015).
3. Dana L. Robert, *American Women in Mission: A Social History of Their Thought and Practice* (Macon, GA: Mercer University Press, 1996), 230.
4. Quoted in James Karanja, *The Missionary Movement in Colonial Kenya: The Foundation of Africa Inland Church* (Göttingen: Cuvillier Verlag, 2009), 92–93.
5. Janice Boddy, *Civilizing Women: British Crusades in Colonial Sudan* (Princeton, NJ: Princeton University Press, 2007), 243.
6. Nina Strochlic, "The U.S. Female Genital Mutilation Crisis," February 6, 2015, www.thedailybeast.com/articles/2015/02/06/female-genital-mutilation-skyrockets-in-the-u-s.html (accessed August 11, 2015).

7. Clover Hope, "President Obama Delivers an Intense Grammys PSA on Domestic Abuse," February 8, 2015, http://jezebel.com/president-obama-delivers-an-intense-grammys-psa-on-dome-1684590013 (accessed August 11, 2015).

8. Richard Land, "Was the Apostle Paul a Misogynist?" February 27, 2015, www.christianpost.com/news/was-the-apostle-paul-a-misogynist-134803/ (accessed August 11, 2015).

9. Pearl S. Buck, *The Exile* (New York: Reynal & Hitchcock, 1936), 283.

10. Dorothy L. Sayers, "The Human-Not-Quite-Human," in *Are Women Human? Penetrating, Sensible, and Witty Essays on the Role of Women in Society* (Grand Rapids: Eerdmans, 2005), 68.

CHAPTER 9: FIFTY SHADES OF RAPE

1. Saint Augustine, *The City of God*, book 1, chap. 19, www.newadvent.org/fathers/120101.htm (accessed August 11, 2015).

2. Laura Stampler, "The (Un)Speakability of Rape: Shakespeare's Lucrece and Lavinia" (Stanford University Honors Thesis, May 14, 2010), 25.

3. Ibid., 24, 28.

4. William Shakespeare, *The Poems: Venus and Adonis, The Rape of Lucrece, The Phoenix and the Turtle, The Passionate Pilgrim, A Lover's Complaint*, ed. John Roe (1992; repr., New York: Cambridge University Press, 2006), 212.

5. Cited in Igor Volsky, "Todd Akin's Pathetic Attempt to Defend 'Legitimate Rape' Goes Down in Flames," July 17, 2014, http://thinkprogress.org/election/2014/07/17/3461252/todd-akins-pathetic-attempt-to-defend-legitimate-rape-goes-down-in-flames/ (accessed August 11, 2015).

6. Samantha Coerbell, "The Romanticization," *The International Journal of Multicultural Studies* 7.1 (Fall–Winter 1999), www.colorado.edu/journals/standards/V7N1/POETRY/coerbell3.html (accessed August 11, 2015).

7. Mimi Haddad, "Fifty Shades of Grey: A Trilogy of Deceit, Collusion, and Domination," February 14, 2015, http://www.

cbeinternational.org/resources/article/fifty-shades-grey?page=show (accessed August 11, 2015).

8. Cited in Susan Estrich, *Real Rape* (Cambridge, MA: Harvard University Press, 1987), 72.

9. Lizzie Crocker, "Virginia Legislator Running for Congress Says Spousal Rape Should Be Legal," January 16, 2014, www.thedailybeast.com/articles/2014/01/16/virginia-legislator-running-for-congress-says-spousal-rape-should-be-legal.html (accessed August 11, 2015).

10. Quoted in Rachel Held Evans, "The Gospel Coalition, Sex, and Subordination," July 18, 2012, http://rachelheldevans.com/blog/gospel-coalition-douglas-wilson-sex (accessed August 11, 2015).

11. J. Lee Grady, "The Dark Side of Wives Submitting to Husbands," August 7, 2013, www.charismamag.com/blogs/fire-in-my-bones/7229-the-dark-side-of-submission (accessed August 11, 2015).

12. Bethan Lloyd-Jones, *Memories of Sandfields* (Edinburgh: Banner of Truth, 1983), 9, www.carolbrandt.com/wp-content/uploads/2012/06/Martyn-Lloyd-Jones.pdf (accessed August 11, 2015).

13. Quoted in Michael A. G. Haykin, *The Christian Lover: The Sweetness of Love and Marriage in the Letters of Believers* (Lake Mary, FL: Reformation Trust, 2009), 86–87.

CHAPTER 10: RISKY OR RELIABLE?

1. Terry A. Moore, "Couples Counseling: Putting Victims Directly in Harm's Way," www.abuseeducation.org/couples_counseling.pdf (accessed August 11, 2015).

2. John Piper, "Clarifying Words on Wife Abuse," December 19, 2012, www.desiringgod.org/articles/clarifying-words-on-wife-abuse (accessed August 11, 2015).

3. Ibid.

4. Quoted in Kathryn Joyce, "Biblical Battered Wife Syndrome: Christian Women and Domestic Violence," June 18, 2009, http://

religiondispatches.org/biblical-battered-wife-syndrome-christian-women-and-domestic-violence/ (accessed August 11, 2015).

5. James Carville and Mary Matalin, *Love and War* (New York: Penguin, 2013).

6. Andrew Malcolm, "Dear Abby: How Do Mary Matalin and James Carville Stay Married without Homicide?" December 27, 2009, http://latimesblogs.latimes.com/washington/2009/12/mary-matalin-james-carville-marriage.html (accessed August 11, 2015).

CHAPTER 11: TWO TO TANGO?

1. Arienne Thompson, "Meredith Vieira Reveals History of Domestic Violence, Explains Why She Stayed," September 17, 2014, http://entertainthis.usatoday.com/2014/09/17/meredith-vieira-reveals-past-abusive-relationship-explains-why-she-stayed/ (accessed August 11, 2015).

2. Ibid.

3. Ibid.

4. Ibid.

5. Elsa Walsh, *Divided Lives: Public and Private Struggles of Three American Women* (New York: Anchor, 1995).

6. Cited in Martin Chilton, "Charles Dickens—the 'Abuser' of Women?" February, 6, 1012, *Telegraph*, http://www.telegraph.co.uk/culture/charles-dickens/9055188/Charles-Dickens-the-abuser-of-women.html (accessed August 11, 2015).

7. Cited in Charles H. Jones, *A Short Life of Charles Dickens with Selections from His Letters* (New York: Appleton, 1880), 200.

8. Essie Fox, "Charles Dickens and His Women," February 7, 2014, http://virtualvictorian.blogspot.com/2012/02/charles-dickens-and-his-women.html (accessed August 11, 2015).

9. Cited in A. B. Hopkins, *Elizabeth Gaskell, Her Life and Work* (London: Lehmann, 1952), 152.

10. Cited in Judith Johnston, "Women and Violence in Dickens' *Great Expectations*," *Sydney Studies* 18 (1992): 96, http://openjournals.library.usyd.edu.au/index.php/SSE/article/view/482/455 (accessed August 11, 2015).

11. Charles Dickens, *Great Expectations* (Harmondsworth: Penguin, 1965), 147.
12. Johnston, "Women and Violence," 104.
13. Times Staff Writer, "O.J. Simpson White Bronco Chase: How It Happened, Minute by Minute," *Los Angeles Times*, June 17, 2014, http://touch.latimes.com/#section/-1/article/p2p-80536397/ (accessed August 11, 2015).

CHAPTER 12: VOWS OF MUTUALITY

1. Jean-Paul Sartre, *Existentialism and Human Emotions* (New York: Kensington, 1987), 23.
2. Michael J. Sullivan, *Heir of Novron* (New York: Orbit, 2012), 737.

11 4712

CPSIA information can be obtained at www.ICGtesting.com
Printed in the USA
LVOW07s2001220316

480318LV00004B/4/P